The Ten Pillars
of a
Happy Relationship

By Jennifer-Crystal Johnson

Jennifer-Crystal Johnson © 2013

ISBN-10: 0985902841
ISBN-13: 978-0-9859028-4-1

Published by:

Broken Publications
PO Box 685
Eatonville, WA 98328

www.brokenpublications.com
jen@brokenpublications.com

Book cover by:

Jennifer-Crystal Johnson
www.jennifercrystaljohnson.com

Broken
Publications

A
Pacific Northwest
Publisher

www.BrokenPublications.com

Other Books by Jennifer-Crystal Johnson:

The Outside Girl: Perception is Reality (PublishAmerica, 2005)

Napkin Poetry (Broken Publications, 2010)

Strangers with Familiar Faces (Broken Publications, 2011)

If You're Human Don't Open the Door (Broken Publications, 2012)

Acknowledgments

A big thank you goes out to everyone I've known who has taught me about relationships, in good ways or bad, firsthand or through observation. Without you, this book would not be possible.

I'd also like to say thanks to everyone who took time out of their busy lives to read the book before publication, give me feedback, and write testimonials. I appreciate it so much, and without you, this book wouldn't be its best.

Thank you!

I'd also like to thank my personal experiences, good and bad, for everything that they have taught me. I believe these collective lessons help me to not only be a better person and a better mother, but also lead a happier life overall.

To my children:

I hope that your path to true and lasting love is much straighter
than mine.

To my parents:

Thanks for showing me the way it should be.

Table of Contents

The Ten Pillars of a Happy Relationship
Jennifer-Crystal Johnson

Maintaining a solid relationship is a skill set – it's not some magical, elusive element that only a few people have or know about. Learning these skills can take a lifetime of "failed" relationships (the way I learned); or, they can be acquired through reading, secondhand experience, and real-life practice. Hopefully this book will help you learn some of these skills and practice them with your current or future partner.

Introduction

Everyone wants to be loved. As a matter of fact, it's probably more than a mere "want." It's a human need to love and be loved. We all crave affection, companionship, and mutual understanding. We all enjoy feeling connected to someone and that internal sensation involving your heart feeling like it's swelling, eyes brimming with happy tears, in-the-moment, complete joy. Those are the moments you know you really love someone.

Who am I and do I even know what I'm talking about? Well, I like to think I do, but I'm not a counselor or psychologist (although I did consider taking that as my major in college), nor am I a relationship "expert." I'm just a single mother of three who runs a business from home and loves to write. I've also been in a lot of relationships of the romantic variety – married and separated by the age of 20 because of domestic violence and a ton of flops and foibles in the years since. I've been in abusive relationships (the bad end of the spectrum) and in very happy relationships (which ended for a variety of reasons unrelated to abuse). I also try to learn from my mistakes – granted it would be easier to learn from secondhand experience, but I guess I like doing things the hard way – which is where I picked up some of the lessons I'm about to share with you.

You can read for fun or take any suggestions that apply… either way, I hope you enjoy, like, share quotes, send comments, and – most importantly – learn or gain perspective. This is the viewpoint of someone who has seen the right way to go about it as well as the wrong way, through observation and experience. Basic psychology is applicable for the entirety of this topic, as well as some more in-depth insights that I've picked up along the way that fall into the personal development category.

I ask that you think of this not as a guide to having a happy relationship but more as a book of suggestions based on experiences and tough life lessons learned through "failure" (I hate that word… let's say challenges instead). It's always easier to look at things from an objective point of view when you aren't too close to a situation, which is why I'm writing this while being single. I firmly believe in the saying that you can't see the forest for the trees, so any time I am able to take a step back and look at the bigger picture, I like to take advantage of it.

I'm leaving physical attraction out of it because that is a given – the first thing to come is physical attraction when you see someone. I'll be focusing on more internal topics that will help build a happy relationship and hopefully offer some insights about why people overreact, get angry, and essentially treat the very people they love so badly at times.

The first internal topic that I want to cover here in the introduction is the reason I'm calling it The Ten Pillars of a *Happy* Relationship, not of a "successful" relationship. Success is very relative and often has a set-in-stone meaning for people, even though the meaning of success is different for everyone. Most people associate success with money, and even I lean toward that at times.

Because success is a term that tends to be pretty stiff for most people, I chose to go with happy as this is much more pliable. Happiness is a feeling, an emotion – success is often viewed as something external. If I say, "successful relationships," do I mean those that work well as a partner unit? Those who have well-earning careers? Those who have nice homes, don't argue in public, and travel regularly? To some people success means mastering gratitude or some step on their path to enlightenment. Do I mean that when I say success? No one would know my definition because everyone's definition is different. This is not a new observation.

However, when I say "happy relationship," I mean just that: happy. Happiness is a feeling everyone has experienced and can relate to, even if they haven't felt that way consistently. Happiness is attainable; some people who are perfectionistic may not see a "successful" relationship as something they can have. But a happy relationship – that is everyone's goal if they choose to be with someone. No one wants to be miserable with someone; if they wanted to *feel* alone or miserable in a relationship, it would be better to just *be* alone, wouldn't it? That's what I've always thought. If I'm going to feel alone, I might as well just be alone.

This difference is something that I've thought about for a long time because I know that success means different things for everyone… and I also know that happiness is something everyone wants and isn't necessarily sure how to get, especially when it comes to relationships.

Hopefully this book will also shed some light on how to help your partner to improve when you know improvement is needed. Of course, having them read this book will help, but there are a number of people who have no interest in reading, which is unfortunate. However, this book outlines ten of the most important things about happy relationships and will allow you to easily share an overview of each section with your loved one. If you're currently single, that's even better – the next time you become involved with someone, have them read this book in the beginning of the relationship while they're still eager to please you and haven't gotten too comfortable yet. Trust me, even if they don't usually read but are trying to impress you, they'll read it. That's the nature of infatuation.

Relationships are an amazing, beautiful thing and can be happy for a long time. It just takes a little effort on the parts of both partners to make that happen. If you have a partner who isn't necessarily all about effort, then maybe it's time that certain ingrained opinions and mindsets be adjusted on their part for a more positive outcome overall. Everyone can change their habits if they choose to do so.

The First Pillar: Learn to Love You First

"You have to love yourself because no amount of love from others is sufficient to fill the yearning that your soul requires from you." –Dodinsky

This is the very first thing that you need to do if you are trying to build a happy relationship. If you can't love yourself, how can you expect someone else to love you? If you don't enjoy your own company, how can you expect someone else to enjoy your company? Consider this section your crash-course on self-esteem and, if you need more help after that, I recommend reading *110 Ways to Boost Your Self-Esteem* and *110 Ways to Change Your Mind* by Henriette Eiby Christensen.

Making peace with who you are and getting to your own happiness is something everyone should do regardless of whether they're taken or single. There are certain steps to becoming happier that anyone can take. It's all internal work; no one can do this for you except you.

If you're looking for a relationship because you think it will make you happy, you'll be disappointed within a short amount of time. Imagine your happiness as a cup full of water. Your cup is full and you're fine, but then you begin to drink that water and deplete it. You find someone else whose cup is full and ask them to share a little with you. If they share too much, their own supply is depleted. Depending on how good you are at being happy by yourself, you will either learn to refill your own cup or you will forever have to share a cup or go back and forth, trading off with your partner so your happiness happens in shifts because neither of you has learned to refill your own happiness cup.

"Don't put the key to your happiness in someone else's pocket – keep it in your own." –Unknown

As an example of this idea, let me share a story from my own experience. I was once with someone who constantly needed to receive validation, even if he simply did something small and mundane like a load of dishes in the dishwasher. If he didn't receive praise for it – and a simple "thank you" was often not enough praise – then he would get completely depressed about it and feel unappreciated and unloved. This isn't exactly the same as happiness, but it's very similar. It got to the point where I was so annoyed with the constant need for praise that I began joking with him, saying, "Do you want a medal for that ten-minute chore?" trying to gently nudge him toward becoming less co-dependent. The reason it was so irritating to me was because the things he was doing were things I did on a daily basis and didn't get any kind of praise or recognition for: dishes, laundry, cooking meals, bathing children, helping them with homework, working on books or client projects with the kids interrupting every few minutes – no one bothered to thank me for all of my work, and I was doing the work of about three people. The dynamic was unbalanced, and it caused frustration.

This can lead to wondering why. Why is my partner not making me happy? Why don't I feel fulfilled in my relationship? The relationship becomes everything and your lack of happiness becomes your partner's fault because you haven't learned to refill your own cup of happiness; you believe that happiness comes from the outside instead of the inside. This is simply false. True happiness always comes from within; it does not and should not depend solely on other people.

"The greater part of our happiness or misery depends upon our dispositions, and not upon our circumstances."
–Martha Washington

That doesn't mean you can't allow your partner to make you happy; as a matter of fact, when happiness is already present, more happiness is easier to enjoy because you don't *need* it to be refilled. Your own happiness is already there; your partner doing nice things or showing their appreciation just adds another bonus. This bonus is much easier to return if it's appreciated and unexpected.

Another thing about relationships is that one plus one has never equaled one. Your identity and individuality must remain intact for a relationship to be happy. If you lose yourself under the pretense of completing your partner, what good is the relationship? Does your partner even care about you for who you are, or are they simply with you for what you do for them or how you make them feel? Have they shared their own cup of happiness with you, or are you the only one sharing, trying desperately to refill your own cup on your own to meet the demands of a needy partner who constantly has to "borrow" some of your happiness because they can't do it on their own?

This dynamic creates a very unhealthy co-dependence and is not sustainable long-term. It's exhausting… it drains one partner and lets the other go on thinking they don't have to put in any effort of their own to help the relationship. Most of this happens without either partner realizing exactly what's going on until months or years later when they're finally fed up, can't take it anymore, and resentment outweighs love.

Those are some things to think about where relationships are concerned. Now, though, I'd like to take you through the basic steps of becoming happy with yourself and loving *you* for who you are.

Know Yourself

You can't love someone if you don't know them, right? This goes for yourself, too. You have to get to know who you are. What do you enjoy doing? Reading? Watching? Working on? Are there certain foods you don't like? Why don't you like them? Are there certain things you secretly wish someone would do for you? Why? What is it about those things that you enjoy so much?

Are you brave? Shy? Outgoing? Loving? Quiet? Loud? Do you prefer reading romance novels or horror? Why? Do you secretly love romantic comedies? Do you find enjoyment in dramatic movies because it's nice to feel vulnerable every now and then?

Do you enjoy the suspenseful, action-packed scenes in crime thrillers because you like the excitement? Do you love the feeling of being scared to death at a movie when creatures/ghosts/serial killers/zombies attack? Or do you prefer movies about survival?

What about your hobbies? Do you like to draw? Write? Go shooting? Paintballing? Do you enjoy being a part of the community theater? Or do you prefer hunting or fishing? Do you like creating art from raw materials like metal and wood or do you prefer working with paint or clay?

What about your core values? Do you believe in God? Are you a churchgoer or do you prefer to be spiritual in your own way? Are you political? Do you believe in the nuclear family or are you more comfortable in a less traditional setting? How do you feel about political parties? What are the issues you care about most in regard to religion and politics? Are you pro-life or pro-choice? Why?

Ask yourself the following questions in order to gain insight, and then we'll move on to the next step. **Be honest in your answers** and circle the one that best applies to you. Don't worry; no one will see these if you don't want them to. This is just for you to get to know yourself better. Some of these may feel a little uncomfortable, but push through anyway – you'll be glad you did.

Do you feel good when you're alone?

Always   Most of the time   Sometimes   Never

Do you get along with others easily?

Always   Most of the time   Sometimes   Never

Are you an outgoing person?

Always   Most of the time   Sometimes   Never

Are you a shy person?

Always   Most of the time   Sometimes   Never

Do you get depressed?

Always   Most of the time   Sometimes   Never

Do you feel that you do the right thing?

Always   Most of the time   Sometimes   Never

Do you get angry easily?

Always   Most of the time   Sometimes   Never

Do you lie to others?

Always   Most of the time   Sometimes   Never

Do you lie to yourself?

Always   Most of the time   Sometimes   Never

Do you admit your mistakes?

Always   Most of the time   Sometimes   Never

Do you feel comfortable apologizing to others?

Always   Most of the time   Sometimes   Never

Do you consider yourself to be an emotional person?

Always   Most of the time   Sometimes   Never

Do you turn to logic and reason when confronted with a problem?

Always   Most of the time   Sometimes   Never

When a problem arises, do you try to find solutions quickly?

Always   Most of the time   Sometimes   Never

Do you consider yourself a patient person?

Always   Most of the time   Sometimes   Never

Next, I'd like you to answer some open-ended questions for further insight. Take your time; you can write these directly in the book or you can choose to use a notebook or journal. Don't think too much about it – it's better to simply answer them with the first answers you arrive at honestly. Again, it's important to be honest with yourself when answering these questions.

1. When do you feel you're at your absolute best on a regular basis?

The Ten Pillars of a Happy Relationship
Jennifer-Crystal Johnson

2. What do you prefer to do when you're alone and why?

3. Are you afraid of being alone, in the moment or in the long run? Why?

4. If you have nothing to do, what do you usually end up doing?

21

5. When you seek out employment, what are the main three things you look for in the job or the company?

Your answers to these questions can give you a lot of insight into your life and where you're headed. I made them open-ended so you truly think about them; don't hold back. Be honest with yourself above all else. If you aren't honest with yourself, then what good will this exercise or any like it do? Absolutely zero. The reason I'm stressing this so much is because lying to yourself can cause a great deal of damage to how much you trust yourself, how you speak to yourself, and how you treat other people in your life, especially your loved ones.

Once you've answered these questions, ask yourself if you're happy with your answers. Is this who you want to be or is it just a stepping stone to who you are becoming? If you feel that there are any issues with your answers or there's anything you want to change about them, figure out what you can change, how you can change it, and take the first step to doing so today. Keep in mind that everything is a process and nothing is ever permanent; no situation, scenario, or emotion is ever there forever.

Everything is temporary. Knowing this helps to put things in perspective and allows you to keep calm and carry on.

I don't have a nervous breakdown or get stressed out at things going wrong, and my quality of life is – in my opinion – very good. I enjoy it! I love the benefits I have on a daily basis by living with a mindset like this.

In order to achieve happiness from the inside, you must re-condition your thought patterns, which begins by recognizing negative thoughts and replacing them with thoughts of gratitude, love, and joy. Do the things that make you happy as often as you can. Meditate. Take some extra time to experience little things in slow motion, taking in scents, sounds, textures, and feelings invoked by whatever it is that you're doing. In other words, stop to smell the roses! If you live a very fast-paced life, you may feel like everything is passing you by. Take five minutes or more out of each day and just slow down for a little bit. Notice how you feel, what you're thinking, and whether you feel fulfilled or not. This can be accomplished in as little or as much time as you choose; there are even ways to meditate for one minute at a time. Even if your life is hectic, happiness is possible.

Some little things you can do for yourself to help get you on your way:

• Meditate. Practice being mindful and aware of yourself, your body, your immediate surroundings, what sounds you hear, and always come back to focus on your slow and steady breathing to keep your thoughts tethered to the here and now.

• Do something that makes you feel good and relaxed at the same time. Paint, draw, listen to your favorite music, write, go for a short drive, eat a bowl of ice cream, take an extra-long shower, give yourself a pedicure, sit outside in the sun and have a beer (or iced tea or coffee if you don't drink alcohol), sing, dance, clean a room in your house, rearrange the furniture, shampoo your carpets – any of these little tasks can help shift your thoughts back to happiness and serenity, especially if you're just beginning your journey.

• Get out of your head. If you tend to be introverted or focus on your thoughts too closely, you can easily get stuck on a handful of negative thoughts and blow them up to five times their original size without even realizing you're doing it. Most people refer to this self-induced depression as "thinking too much" to make it sound better and like they have no control over it. I'm here to let you know that you *do* have control over your thoughts, and your thoughts heavily influence your emotions. If you don't take control of this, you're inviting nothing but chaos and chances are you won't do very well in a relationship with someone else simply because you haven't learned how to have a good relationship with yourself.

You can change anything you have control over, including your own emotions and thought processes. You can change your mindset. And when you learn how to change your mindset and maintain control over your own emotions, you will be well on your way to happiness from the inside out.

Accept Yourself

Once you get to know yourself a little bit, it's time to accept what you can and change what you're unable or unwilling to accept. There are solutions to every problem you could possibly have… some of these solutions won't be easy, so if you choose not to take the necessary actions to change what you aren't happy with, then you have no one to blame but yourself. This is an important part of taking responsibility for yourself, your life, and your emotions. It sounds harsh now (it sounded harsh to me the first time I heard it, too), but once you begin practicing some of these techniques, it will become a phrase of empowerment.

I'll let you in on a little secret about making changes. You can literally talk yourself out of doing *anything* by making excuses, justifying a lack of action by citing risks, complaining that the risks aren't worth the potential rewards, going into lazy mode and dreading the work involved in the process (procrastination), and many other tactics that take place either in your mind or in conversation when you have a big decision to make or some kind of journey to undertake, like achieving a goal. You can literally talk yourself out of anything, even if you know it's the best thing for you to do. Even if you know you need to do it. Your thoughts, if not controlled or harnessed properly by you, can and will hold you back more than anything or anyone else in this life.

How do you overcome this?

Take action before those thoughts have time to enter into your mind. I'll give you an example of something I struggle with on a daily basis: cleaning the house. As a single mom of three working from home, it's extremely important for me to be able to work, but I can't focus if there's a mess all around me. I can if I try to shut it out, but it's very difficult. The problem is that the mess-makers tend to grumble about helping me clean, which sometimes leads them to simply avoiding the task all together instead of simply getting up and doing it. I know they get this from me; I've done the same thing. And once this attitude is a habit, it becomes much more difficult to break out of.

When I look around and I see my house in "disarray" (usually it's more like a paper hurricane hit it, followed by a herd of pets who may or may not have overeaten and thrown up that day, followed by some kind of cookie monster creature because crumbs appear seemingly out of nowhere, followed by a laundry monster who likes to throw everything on the floor to confuse me about what's clean and what's dirty), I look around and my heart sinks. I start thinking, "Ok. I have to continue doing laundry, then vacuum, then shampoo the carpets because what in the world are those stains? Then sweep, mop, clean the bathroom, vacuum out the couches, wash the rugs, vacuum the stairs and possibly shampoo those, too, completely replace all the cat litters, do the dishes, clean the counters and maybe the walls in the kitchen because there's goo all over the wall where the trash can is, and did my son really color all over the walls again? Why is his bedroom door broken? Why are there little stab marks in the wall in the hallway? Now I have to fill wall holes and repaint again…. How did he get scissors and what did he use them on? Oh crap, there goes his window screen…. At least he didn't throw his sisters' blankets and toys out of their window again."

You can see how this would become overwhelming on a daily – we'll be conservative and say weekly – basis. Kids are crazy! And mine happen to be somewhat destructive (I attribute this partially to boredom and partially to a need for creative outlet on whatever they happen to find). Your own experiences with this may vary, but I'm sure kids all over the world do things that make us grown-ups just shake our heads in disbelief (I know I did!).

What I do when I'm most productive and happy is I don't even think about everything I need to do. I pick one task immediately – usually the first thing I see – and do it as efficiently as possible. Music helps. I don't think while I'm cleaning; I kind of try to let my mind go blank and focus on the task at hand. Cleaning is mindless. This is a wonderful relief from my thought-intensive line of work and requires attention to detail, but not in the same way as editing or writing a book does. Cleaning is like my brain's vacation, and music makes it fun. Loud music, of course! Listening to quiet music while cleaning is like rappelling off of a ten-foot boulder. It just doesn't satisfy.

When I ask my kids to do something for me, they already know that I mean now. Don't dawdle, don't wait until the TV show is over, do it NOW. This helps to get them past that thought process, and usually, if I tell them I need it done immediately, they do it without question. They never like it... but they do it without getting a chance to think too much about why they don't want to.

The point of this illustration? JUST DO IT. Don't think about what you have to do before you get started on it because it will deter you, it will make it more difficult to start, and it will slow you down massively. If you want to make changes in order to accept and eventually love yourself for who you are, you must begin taking action toward those changes immediately. Those actions always sound worse than what they actually are – like cleaning or even exercising for example – but if you don't just do it, you will keep thinking about why you don't want to and then it simply won't get done. The procrastination monster takes over.

This same kind of thinking is exactly what writer's block is, too. There is no such thing as writer's block... there is only justifying not writing because it seems too hard or too challenging or too tedious or whatever the logic might be. If you do as Nike says and just do it, things become much simpler and you no longer need to pep-talk yourself to get a move on.

Why am I going on and on about this? Because change is difficult for a lot of people. In fact, many people fear change of any kind. Many people don't want to even think about anything changing *ever* because the unknown is often scarier than staying the same. Staying the same has become comfortable. Changing means making yourself uncomfortable, and who wants to be uncomfortable? Unfortunately, it is necessary in order to succeed in life and do anything that you know needs to be done, even if you don't want to.

> "But I'm good at being uncomfortable so I can't stop changing all the time."
> –Fiona Apple, Extraordinary Machine

If you need to practice this concept, practice it first with house chores or small tasks that you have to do on a regular basis and hate doing. For me, it's folding laundry. UGH – I absolutely *loathe* folding laundry, but I know it needs to be done, period, otherwise I end up washing the same clothes over and over without ever wearing them because the kids or the cats do something to mess them up.

Instead of letting yourself think about it, do it as soon as it pops into your mind. Drop whatever else you're doing for a few minutes (unless you absolutely can't, in which case you should plan to do it at a specific time or right after you're done with your current task and stick to that plan *no matter what*) and don't allow those thoughts to take over. Instead, just get on it and get it done – it's really not as bad as your brain tells you it's going to be.

Once you've done this a few times, it begins becoming a habit to *just do* instead of letting your thoughts stop you. So now, you're ready for something a little bigger and more challenging, right?

Whatever it is about you that you don't like and want to change can be changed with less emotional effort once you've practiced a little bit. It may or may not be hard work depending on what you're changing, but the emotional barriers of resistance that everyone tends to set up have now been toppled by a new action-oriented thought process that makes just doing something easier than meandering around it for hours.

When I was younger, I remember my mom sitting down with my brother to do homework and he would argue, negotiate, cry, fight, throw a tantrum, and try to weasel his way out of doing the homework for hours. For hours they would sit there at the dining room table, mother trying to get son to make even a single pencil mark, and he would try anything and everything he could to get out of it.

If he had simply done it in the first place, he would've had those hours to play.

If you just do what you need to do without thinking about it, your days will be way more productive and your free time will increase because you're doing what you need to do quickly, working toward your goals, and then just being done with it.

So let's say the thing you want to change is something that will take a long time, like losing a substantial amount of weight. You obviously can't do this quickly – it could take a year or two before you get to the point where you want to be. Don't worry – you won't hate that part about you forever and I can tell you why.

First, your appearance doesn't represent you in your entirety. People are so complex! You can feel like you know someone extremely well and then *bam!* You find out they had some dark secret in their past or a weird quirk about their personality you never knew about for years. It happens all the time! And not always in a negative way, either. Sometimes it's just something really weird or even something good.

So no; your physical appearance, especially something as changeable as weight, does not define you and you should not let it. If it's a big deal to you, everyone you meet will sense that and suddenly it's a big deal to them, too. Aside from that, if you're looking for a happy relationship and your concern is that you're overweight, then think about this next idea.

I have been on both sides of the weight issue. I have been thin and I have been fat. The only reason it doesn't bother me either way is because I'm tall and can carry an extra 50 pounds without people taking much notice. Once it gets to an extra 100, though, it gets to be uncomfortable for me.

However, I tend to look at it this way. If attraction and then love is real and the person is more interested in your personality than your looks – which could be a dangerous thing because they could just want to sleep with you and nothing more, and how would you tell the difference unless you're good at reading people – then there might be a future there. However, if the person is more interested in your body and what you look like, it could very well just be lust, and then what? Potential STDs, disappointment, and the search goes on for the next one while you try to remember you're worth more than just sex. Believe me, some guys try for weeks to get into a girl's pants just to avoid her after he succeeds; another notch on the bedpost, so to speak. Some girls are the same exact way.

People can be fickle and superficial; if someone shows no interest in your personality, how would that make you feel? That's where being a little overweight isn't such a bad thing, in my opinion. If someone is talking to you, they usually feel a genuine attraction to your personality as well as your looks, even though your looks may not be ideal by society's standards (or even theirs, for that matter). Mind you this can be applied to girls who everyone says are "too skinny," too – no one likes to be told to go eat a burger because they look too thin. That causes all sorts of weird self-esteem issues, too, but both also offer positive aspects as far as being able to tell if someone is interested just for the physical or if they're interested in a deeper connection.

Having said all of that, I'm pleased to say that you don't have to be at your ideal weight in order to accept yourself. If this is something you absolutely despise about yourself and can't live with, the first steps to changing it will already be enough to point your thoughts in a direction of acceptance. If you're constantly beating yourself up about it, though, it will take longer. Learn to be more positive in how you speak to yourself – instead of telling yourself you're fat or too skinny or stupid or unworthy, reach inside and pull out the truth you know deep down to be the most accurate: You are beautiful. You are worthy. You deserve better, and even if you're not perfect, you are an amazing human being because each and every one of us is a miracle at birth and has a purpose to serve throughout life, should we choose to accept said purpose.

So first, take your action steps every day to make the change you want to. Next, your mindset and the way you think of yourself has to be reconditioned. If you put yourself down all the time, of course you'll start believing it! It's coming from you! I'm not saying to lie to yourself and develop a massive ego – that can be just as unattractive as being insecure.

What I'm saying is to become happy with who you are deep down; become confident. Your personality will make or break you in life. If you're too nice, people walk on you. If you're too mean, no one will want to get close to you. The trick is to know yourself and know who you are; to know what you stand for, what you want, what you feel is right, and to know that you're not acting irrationally or falsely justifying your actions if they're mean-spirited, jealous, or misguided.

Learning to accept who you are is the fastest way to making permanent changes because those changes will be sincere. If you don't accept yourself, any changes you try to make for improvement will be based on a lie to yourself. The universe may not revolve around you, but you are the most important person in your own life. Acceptance of your flaws, your failures, your strengths, your successes, your achievements, your ingrained traits – all of this will propel you forward into loving yourself and leading a happier life, with or without a relationship to help the happiness factor.

Love Yourself

Make it a point to begin appreciating and loving yourself, even if you're not exactly where you want to be in life or in the way you look. Remember: everything is temporary. The present is simply a stepping stone to your future, and what you choose to do with it is up to you.

Having said that, there are some simple things you can do in order to feel more loving toward yourself. I'll cover this in more detail later in the book, but being grateful is always an excellent place to start.

For example, if the main issue you have is with your appearance, go look in a mirror. Begin by picking and choosing what you *like* about yourself. Your skin, your eyes, your size, your hair… your lips, your smile, your teeth… it can be anything. For me, it's my eyes, teeth, hair, and skin. And who cares about the rest for now? Just focus on those things that you like about the way you look. If you're a woman, put on some makeup if you need to. Do your hair. Brush your teeth. Accentuate the parts you love and play down the parts you don't. If you can change the things you don't like, then create an action plan to begin changing those things. If you can't, then work on accepting it and appreciating it anyway.

If you don't like your teeth, remember that there are people in the world who have no teeth and can't afford to get work done to fix that. If you don't like your eyes, keep in mind that there are people in the world who can't even see. If you don't like your feet, keep in mind that some people only have one leg – or none. Now imagine how grateful and appreciative someone worse off than you would be if they could trade places with you. Really feel that emotion of gratitude and appreciation. Imagine it being you who can't see, or has no teeth, or has only one leg. Imagine how much more difficult life would be for you if that were you. Then come back and look again. It really doesn't seem so bad now, does it?

For an incredibly inspirational story, look up No Arms, No Legs, No Worries! Nick Vujicic still lives an incredibly full and wonderful life and inspires others to do the same. It's absolutely incredible, and if you have any qualms about yourself physically, this is someone who can help change your perspective. His videos are free on YouTube.

Another way to love yourself is to take good care of yourself physically, emotionally, and spiritually. Shower or take baths often (if you've ever become a mother, you know how easy it can be to fall into neglecting this necessity with a newborn, especially if you're by yourself with no one to babysit). Do something you massively enjoy for at least 30 minutes a day. Listen to music you love – you'll be amazed how much music can lift your mood and your emotional state. If you pray, pray daily. If you meditate, meditate daily. If you love to sing, do that daily. If you enjoy dancing, do that daily. If you love to write, do that daily.

It's little things like this that add up to a more fulfilling life experience – and more happiness. Your happiness is your responsibility; we all know we have no control over anyone else (at least I hope people know that by now), so we must take control of *ourselves*. If we don't take control over ourselves, we end up becoming controlling and abusive to others because we blame everything and everyone else for how we feel when this is the furthest thing from the truth.

"Everything else you see and experience in this world is effect, and that includes your feelings. The cause is always your thoughts." –Rhonda Byrne, *The Secret*

The key thing to remember about loving yourself is this: whatever you think and feel toward yourself, you will get more of. If you feel like you hate some of your behavior, your unconscious mind will automatically take that feeling and make it last longer, be louder, and stay persistent, as well as attracting people into your life who think those same things about you or themselves. However, if you choose to chase those feelings away and replace them with more positive feelings, your unconscious mind will amplify those and make them brighter and more persistent... and attract people into your life who will more easily accept you and themselves.

You've had the necessary tools within you to accomplish all of this all along. You've just never used them (or maybe you have); they're still in the package, shiny and clean and ready to serve their purpose whenever you decide to finally open them up and go for it.

Trust Yourself

Trusting yourself involves several things. First, you must be aware of your own thoughts, feelings, behaviors, and actions, as well as how they affect you and others over the short- and long-term. Second, you must take responsibility for those thoughts, feelings, behaviors, and actions. Third, you must be honest with yourself, even if it's painful. This is a pretty big obstacle to overcome, but it becomes much easier once you do it once or twice because you learn the benefits of it. Last but not least, you must be willing to trust your instincts, even if they aren't always logical or rational, and recognize them as an opportunity.

Please don't confuse instincts with impulses, as they are extremely different. Impulses are based solely on wants, whether they're good or bad. Child molesters, rapists, and murderers have bad impulses, for example. Where impulses usually conflict with your core values, instincts are harmonious with them. Knowing your core values, you may have an impulse to sleep with someone and have a one night stand; but instinctively, you may decide not to because you get a funny feeling about the other person that may put you in danger.

Long story short? Impulses are usually bad while instincts are usually good. Have you ever heard of a store setting up an instinct-shopping rack near the register? Probably not. That's why it's called impulse buying.

The biggest difference between impulses and instincts is that impulses are usually triggered by an external stimulus while instincts are ingrained and honed throughout our lives and why our "gut feelings" become stronger and more accurate as we get older. Our past experiences and how we deal with and view them afterward help to hone our instincts. Interestingly, we also become more adept at controlling our impulses as we get older. A teenager will be more susceptible to making bad decisions based on what they want right now than a grown person who has overcome the instant gratification mindset.

This is another area of life where paying attention to your own thoughts, emotions, feelings, and actions comes into play. One of the most important parts of paying attention is to be honest with yourself, especially if you're serious about being the best person you can be. This requires becoming aware and willing to admit when your behavior or thoughts are less than stellar (you're not alone if they ever have been or ever are … no one is perfect).

Self-awareness is a term I learned at about 21 while working as a leasing specialist in an apartment complex. One of the older residents came to the office to chat and asked me, "When did you first become self-aware?"

"What do you mean?" I asked her, a little puzzled because I'd never heard that word before.

"Well," she explained, "you seem extremely mature – how old are you?"

"21," I said, not surprised at seeming mature as I'd been mistaken for a teacher at 13 and as 26 at age 15 and 17.

"Wow, you're so young! What I mean by self-aware is that you have a good understanding of yourself and why you do the things you do."

I smiled at the elderly woman and said, "Thank you." I had just left an abusive marriage, so to hear a compliment like that was a big deal for me at the time.

"I bet people tell you all the time you're an old soul," she added, and we laughed a little, moving on to the next topic.

Self-awareness is not self-consciousness or self-esteem. It has little or nothing to do with either. Now that we know what it isn't, let's look at what it is.

Being self-aware is partially having the presence to catch yourself when you're doing something or saying something that isn't coming from the best place within yourself. One of the things I struggle with as far as this goes is yelling at my kids. It's easy to blame them for my reaction, but deep down I know that it isn't their fault. It isn't them. It's 100% me; I have the ability to react differently and therefore it's my responsibility to recognize it and change it. Self-awareness means putting on the brakes when you catch yourself in a bad habit and regrouping. Self-awareness means having the willingness and learned ability to see yourself from another perspective – the perspective of the best you within or the people around you (and how they may be feeling as a result of your words or actions) – and act on that perspective to become a better person.

Just being aware of your own behaviors and habits is a huge step toward becoming the best person you can be. If you catch yourself biting your nails, that's the first step to breaking that habit because you can do something else instead of biting your nails the second you realize you're doing it or are about to. Keep your hands busy. Or, as a character in a book I once read used to do, sit on your hands.

To give you a better idea of self-awareness and getting to it, I want to go over the four stages of awareness with you. These are shared and documented on a number of websites online if you'd like more information, but I will certainly do my best to explain them briefly.

1. Unconscious Incompetence

Some sayings that apply: "Ignorance is bliss," or, "You don't know what you don't know." Essentially this means that you just don't know any better because you haven't gained the knowledge that will help move you forward. This is applicable to business, relationships, and life in general. If you don't know something, how would you know you don't know it? You would have to be introduced to the concept, just like everyone else.

2. Conscious Incompetence

This could be referred to as the "Aha!" moment, when you have an epiphany or come to the realization that you don't know something and want to learn more. This is also referred to as painful awareness and can signal the beginning of the next level.

3. Conscious Competence

This level usually represents people who make an effort to educate themselves by learning through reading and other, more educated people. If you think about it, you can really learn anything from anywhere in the world through books, the internet, courses online, and so on. Learning is an amazing experience, especially if you apply what you learn. I believe this is the level I'm on currently, though I'd like to be at level four.

4. Unconscious Competence

This is when you've learned so much and begun applying it so much that it becomes second nature. Highly successful people do this in their marketing efforts, for example. They've been doing it for so long that it's become a habit.

What does this have to do with trusting yourself? Well… if you become accountable to yourself and catch yourself doing things you know deep down you don't *really* want to do, then you are building that trust with yourself. You are sending yourself the message that you are reliable and dependable as well as learning your own behaviors and habits so you now know what you didn't before.

Taking responsibility for your thoughts, feelings, behaviors, and actions is a bit harder than just being aware of them because it means you have to be held accountable. You cannot blame exterior people or circumstances for your thoughts, feelings, behaviors, or actions because they are all coming from you. YOU are the one thing that every aspect of your life has in common. YOU.

Do you remember when we were kids and played video games, and whenever someone died they would yell, "Look what you made me do!" This is the exact opposite of being accountable for yourself! This is shifting the blame to someone else so you don't have to admit to messing up yourself. Unfortunately, there are millions and millions of people who blame *everything* that goes wrong in their lives on exterior things. It's the economy, it's the weather, it's the kids, it's the boss, it's the other person in the relationship, it's the universe, it's karma, it's punishment from God… none of that is true! Well, maybe karma is. The only reason you believe any of that is true and succumb to it is because you *believe* it's true and succumb to it.

Of course you can't take full control over all of your thoughts. The average person has anywhere between 10,000 to 70,000 thoughts in a day, depending on your sources. Monitoring them would be impossible and taking control over each one is most definitely impossible! But thoughts lead to feelings, which can be used as a sort of compass to guide your thoughts in the right direction. For example, if you think about bad things that might happen if you leave your house today, chances are you'll feel anxious about leaving the house. The trick is to learn how to push those kinds of thoughts aside and go back into a more positive direction in your mind.

If I have to go somewhere and am driving, I may suddenly worry about getting into a car accident. My internal dialogue might look something like this:

Negative: "People get in accidents all the time, and there are a ton of people who don't drive very well, or safely for that matter."

Positive: "Well, I'll just have to pay closer attention, then. I'm a good driver; I have also been a not-so-good driver in the past, so I have experience with what to watch out for. Bonus."

Negative: "What if you can't avoid it?"

Positive: "The best thing to do is be aware of my surroundings and deal with whatever may come if it actually comes. Thinking about 'what if' is pointless and stressful, so I'm going to stop now and enjoy my drive while listening to music and singing my heart out!"

Once I choose to change direction, I usually do something to distract myself from whatever idle worries my brain has conjured up. Oftentimes I'll also pull the law of attraction into it by asking myself if putting so much focus on a scenario that may or may not happen will actually attract that scenario to me. That usually snaps me out of it pretty quickly if reminding myself that worrying about maybes is pointless doesn't.

The way I look at it is that life is stressful enough already. Why put yourself through even more stress – unnecessary stress at that – by worrying about things that haven't happened? I choose to cross bridges when I get to them.

> "'Reality' is the only word in the English language that should always be used in quotation marks."
> –Unknown

Think about that for a minute. This is actually one of my favorite quotes because I learned a long time ago how differently people view the world, life, and themselves. If you tie this together with other quotes and sayings illustrating that perception is reality, the mind conceiving an idea leading to achievement, thinking you can or thinking you can't and being right about it either way, and so on and so forth, suddenly you have this incredible concept of reality that so many want but can't seem to get to. Why is that? It's because they don't believe they can achieve that mindset. Or maybe they don't believe they're worthy of achieving that mindset. They don't want to admit to having the power to change things simply through belief because blaming external things gets them off the hook.

And what does this have to do with trusting yourself? Well, think about it this way:

Joe is an average guy. He works an average job at a factory (this could even be a button factory, if you want, like the kids' rhyme game) and makes enough to get by and still go out for drinks a couple of times a month. Joe, however, feels stuck. It's the same monotony, the same routine, the same boring activities from one day to the next. He hates it. He would like to change things around, but Joe doesn't think he's capable of anything else because this is all he knows. Therefore, he doesn't even try. He has talked himself out of change, even if it would improve his quality of life.

After a while, Joe begins to drink more and more often. He starts to get depressed, gains weight, and becomes angry if anyone asks him if he's okay or tries to help him. He doesn't like to get unsolicited advice, no matter how good the intentions behind it. Joe spirals downward into depression and even more drinking.

While commiserating with others at the bar, he tells people frequently, "My job drives me to drink. I gained weight because I drink and I'm stressed out all the time, so I get mad. I'm depressed now and I don't know why, and all this because of that stupid job!"

Upon getting fired, he says, "I've been there for 10 years! Obviously the boss has something against me. Now I have to find a new job or go on unemployment because of that jerk."

Isn't it more likely that the boss saw Joe getting more and more out of control and fired him so he wouldn't be a liability? I think so. But if Joe were to admit that, then he would have to take responsibility for his own actions. So he blames the boss and gets on with it, feeling bitter and resentful toward his old job as well as his old boss.

That brings me to my next point: honesty. Blaming external things for every problem you have is basically like lying to yourself on a constant basis. Who can trust a liar? No one! Do you trust liars? No? I know I don't. Then why become that which you don't trust – and probably don't even like? I hate being lied to! It's one of the worst things in the world to me personally because I know the truth will always come out one way or another. I'd rather have someone be honest with me and feel hurt than have them lie to me only to find out later because that not only hurts, it also breaks down the trust you have with that person. You can't trust them to tell you something important that you needed to know, so you look at that person in a completely different way. The same thing can happen with yourself.

Now imagine you've been split in half and there are two of you. *Poof!* Magic. You are face to face with yourself. You hang out, watch a movie, chat, laugh, and have a great time. Then you begin to notice something strange. Every time there's a disagreement, the other you blames you for it. When the movie bombs and is a disappointment, it's because you picked it and suck at picking movies. When trivia is disputed and you're right, the other you accuses you of cheating. When the food you cook together turns out terrible, it's automatically your fault. You just can't do anything right!

That's it! You think. *That other me has got to GO!*

This other you lies to avoid taking responsibility and doesn't even realize what's really going on. But you, as you've taken a step back to observe yourself, now see what being honest with yourself really means.

You can't love someone you don't trust, and you can't trust a liar – so I recommend getting straight with yourself as soon as possible, even if that means admitting to not being as excellent or awesome as you would like to be. Remember: everything is temporary and you are a work in progress!

The Second Pillar: Let Go of Fear

It has often been said that you've got to give it everything you have for love. It's also been said that people sometimes fear success or happiness. The first time I read that somewhere, I understood it immediately. One of the biggest reasons people fear things like this is because people fear change. Changing usually takes effort to adjust to, whether that change is a choice or not, and whether that change is positive or not. The adjustment period is still there, and some changes are easier than others.

Changing your habits is the main aspect of this fear of happiness. It isn't the actual happiness itself that people fear, but the process of changing their habits in order to get to that happiness. Someone who constantly complains, for example, may feel that once they stop complaining they won't have anything to talk about. They don't care that vocalizing their complaints over and over again is probably making them twice as miserable as the thing they're complaining about; they just don't want to change that habit because it's (insert excuse here).

You may not even call it fear. You could simply call it nervousness about making changes. Change is hard! But it's the one thing you can count on in life. Things are always changing, always moving, always evolving.

"The only thing that is constant is change." –Heraclitus

Fear is a pretty big issue, even though some people don't even realize it. For example... I used to write only in specific places at specific times of day in my journal. Anywhere else and I suddenly felt blocked, like I wasn't comfortable enough to let it out. One day, someone pointed out to me very sarcastically that if I love to write, I can't wait for the eclipse and the planets to align every time I want to write a poem.

I took those comments to heart and realized that this person was completely right about that. I was afraid that my writing would somehow be different when the atmosphere wasn't "right." Then I realized that my writing is my writing no matter where I write it or what time it is. Sure, there might be minor differences and certain subtle variations, but that's all part of the learning process toward becoming an even better writer, isn't it? It then became an opportunity to know my writing and myself better, as well as to hone my skills based on myself rather than my surroundings. And guess what? My writing was fine.

By now you're probably wondering where I'm going with this, so without further ado, here it is: people fear happiness. People fear trying for a happy relationship because they want to be emotionally prepared for a failure.

"Fear is faith that it won't work out." –Elbert Hubbard

50% of marriages end in divorce, after all. And this is where the mistake happens. Without even realizing what you're doing, you go into a relationship thinking, "Well, at least I know I won't be too devastated if it ends badly." Immediately you're expecting failure and bringing those feelings – that vibe, if you will – into the relationship. This in turn leads to giving your relationship maybe 60-80% of what it needs to grow and thrive, always coming up short. You've essentially set yourself up for failure through your beliefs and mindset.

The real kicker is this: if you had given it 100% without thinking about the end before it began, would it still have failed? I'm no psychic, but I can make an educated guess that a majority of the relationships that this happens to would've at least lasted longer, if not forever – and been happier.

There's an underlying epidemic in our society that is run on fear and fear-based beliefs. Mind you, this all happens underneath our conscious development. Also, it can be changed on an individual basis, so it isn't set in stone. Remember, everything is temporary.

The problem is that fear has all sorts of crazy side-effects and consequences. Ask yourself this: why does every single product have a warning label on it, even if it's something ridiculous that should be common sense? Because the companies creating these products are afraid of being sued and held liable for anything that may happen involving this product. Why do they get sued? Well, in legitimate lawsuits, the people suing oftentimes can't afford the medical treatment they may need. But in frivolous suits where no medical care is needed, it comes down to one thing: people are deathly afraid to take responsibility for their own mistakes. It can be embarrassing to admit to doing something stupid. This is not nature; this is nurture at its best, creating people who, if not made self-aware during their lives, are bound to keep any accountability that could fall on them at bay through whatever means necessary. It is a fear-based habit.

Similarly, look at how over-reactive everyone gets during a crisis. And I don't want to minimize any of the tragedies that have happened, but how many of you remember the Columbine school shooting in Colorado and how everyone began blaming Marilyn Manson's music for the tragedy? Instead of holding the shooters themselves accountable for being twisted and clearly unable to manage their own emotions (for whatever reasons they may have had), people found a scapegoat and blamed a musician whose music is an idea and whose message was meant for pure shock value as an entertainer. An idea cannot carry or fire a gun. Scapegoating is a fear-based habit.

Another more recent fear-based reaction is not allowing little kids to have anything in the shape of a gun whatsoever, no exceptions, even if it's something as harmless as a toaster pastry or their fingers. I personally find this ridiculous because boys especially are naturally drawn to guns, swords, and other weapons as children. Reacting fearfully instead of teaching safety actually does them a disservice. I know not everyone is likely to agree with me on that, but the fact that fear is behind these new rules remains the same.

What does this have to do with happy relationships? Everything!

Would you want to be in a relationship where your partner blamed everything on you even if it was their fault (a fear of taking responsibility or admitting they were wrong)? What about a partner who was constantly worried about you cheating or leaving them and needed validation all the time (a fear that they aren't good enough for happiness or they don't deserve it)? Or how about a relationship where even things beyond anyone's control are your fault according to your partner (severe control issues)? All of these habits, these behaviors, are rooted in fear.

In order to avoid becoming the types of people I just described, you must let go of your own fears, at least for the most part. A healthy sense of fear is fine, but living your life completely drowning in fear and worry isn't good for anyone, especially since most of those types of fears are completely made up in our own minds.

> "Feed your faith and your fears will starve to death."
> –Max Lucado

A few quick tips on letting go of fear:

• Don't entertain unnecessary paranoia. Sure, something *might* go wrong... but do you really want to worry about getting into a car accident every time you drive anywhere? After all, you might get into an accident, right? That doesn't mean you should be overly paranoid on the road, though. Just that paranoia alone might inhibit your driving abilities to the point of getting into an accident because you aren't focused. Think about it.

• Catch and stop yourself if you get caught up in thoughts about "what if" and "if only." You'll drive yourself nuts thinking those!

• No matter what your past looks like, let it go – you can't change it, but you can decide not to let it negatively rule your present. You can also choose to embrace the lessons you've learned from hardship with gratitude and appreciation, as well as a sense of strength because you wouldn't be who you are today without those experiences and the lessons they have taught you.

• Just because you haven't had a lasting relationship yet doesn't mean you've failed. You've just learned a number of ways not to do it. Forgive yourself and move on, learning to be at peace with your decisions and any regret you may have.

• Regret is scarier than a lot of other things in life. If you look back and see yourself having many relationships that ended because you under-committed… well, how do you think you'll feel about that when you're 80?

Begin Letting Go of Your Fears about Relationships

To let go of your fears about relationships, there are a few things you can do to get started and kind of work your way there. The first is to change the way you think about relationships and the opposite gender. Though it's helpful to understand where these fears came from, that isn't the most important aspect.

Maybe you've been cheated on. Maybe you think all men are assholes. Maybe you think all women are emotionally abusive and manipulative. Maybe you think that you're just not cut out to be with anyone. And trust me, at one point or another, I've fallen into generalizing people in some way. I've also learned it isn't helpful… as a matter of fact, it can be very damaging to your first impressions of people because you're closing yourself off to possibilities based on a personal bias.

My personal experience with falling into generalizations about men came from being married to an abuser. My daily worry was whether I was going to piss him off or not. That was all I could think about, and it got to a point where it didn't matter if the house was spotless or dinner was made – if there was even a single basket of clean laundry on the couch, I was in trouble.

According to him, sex was my wifely duty. Whether I wanted to or not, we were having sex every night. I didn't realize that this was rape until way later, and I cried myself to sleep almost nightly.

I used to love guns until he pointed one in my face. After that, it took years for me to get over that fear of guns because I didn't want to get shot.

Death threats were a regular occurrence. "I know a guy who will kill someone for $5,000," he would tell me.

Needless to say, my perception of men changed dramatically after experiencing those things at the hands of someone who said they loved me. Unfortunately, so did my daughter's. However, I realized that I can't go through life generalizing everyone and lumping them into the same category. I can't go through life believing all men are abusive.

"You can conquer almost any fear if you will only make up your mind to do so. For remember, fear doesn't exist anywhere except in the mind." –Dale Carnegie

Remember how we talked about the power of beliefs and how, if you believe something, that becomes your reality? This applies here, too. If you enter into a relationship with the end already in sight, then the end is sure to come. If you enter into it openly and with hope and appreciation, the entire experience is likely to be more positive.

Love, lasting and happy love, takes work, perseverance, and a mutual commitment to put the relationship before individual needs. Of course individual needs should be met, too – but that's where the word "compromise" comes in. For example, I doubt that any person in a relationship, male or female, would appreciate being left home with the kids three to five times a week so their partner can go party at the bar because they claim to "need" it. This is completely imbalanced and has a tendency to breed resentment. Likewise, a balance needs to be struck between the individuals and what they each require from the relationship.

The Four Categories of Balance

In a relationship, there are four basic categories of balance as far as how people spend their time. Obviously work is a part of most people's daily lives; this means that, if your partner is working from home, you shouldn't interrupt them during their work hours. It also means that, if your partner works outside the home, you shouldn't bombard them with information and updates the second they walk in the door. Give them time to wind down, get home fully, maybe change into sweats, and settle in. Usually family meal time is when people have ample opportunity to share their days, which is why many people place such importance on eating dinner together as a family.

Obviously, though, everyone has friends, family, kids, and romantic needs to take care of. So this is where the four categories come in and where a balance can be struck.

1. Family time.
2. Alone time.
3. Romantic time.
4. Social time (friends and/or extended family).

These four elements of balance are covered in more detail in the chapter on balance later in the book, but let's do a quick overview of each one.

Family time is first, so let's look at that a little more closely. Obviously if you have kids in the picture, this would be the time you all spend together doing something as a family.

If you don't have kids and it's just you and your partner, family time could be a time when you focus on getting to know each other better, have a good conversation, or do something non-sexual to maintain that emotional connection and make each other feel like you're still interested in the person you're with and not just the physical needs they provide comfort for.

This is especially directed at men: if your partner stops feeling like you're interested in her and starts feeling like you're only interested in sex, she's not going to be happy about it. Instead of feeling loved, she's more likely to feel used. This is something to keep in mind when making an effort to maintain a happy relationship.

Alone time is next, and honestly this is a bigger deal to some people than others. There's absolutely nothing wrong with enjoying some time to yourself.

Alone time can be an important piece of the puzzle. This is simply because no two people, no matter how close they are or how well they get along, can be around each other or do everything together without needing a little space after a while. Trust me; I've tried! And I *still* love my alone time.

Alone time simply means that: time to yourself. To do whatever you damn well please (without hurting anyone, of course – this should be a given, but you never know in a society where people need warning labels announcing that a caped costume will not give the wearer the ability to fly) for a while. The amount of alone time needed will differ from one person to the next.

The main thing here is to be okay with your partner spending time by themselves without flying off the handle about how that somehow means they don't love you. That's an immature, jealous reaction, so in order to have a happy relationship, immature and jealous behaviors should be managed and minimized through self-awareness.

Next on our short list is romantic time! This need will probably vary from one individual to the next, too, and definitely varies between genders. Guys, you would be surprised what a little romance can do for your attractiveness factor. Ladies, you'll be surprised what a little romance will do for your insecurity levels.

Let me elaborate just a little bit on this. Romance shouldn't happen *all the time* because something that happens all the time loses its impact. For example, if you hear someone tell you they love you all day long, you begin to doubt it because they say it so often. Just like if you hear someone constantly apologizing, it loses its meaning because – guess what – next thing you know, there's another thing this person did that they need to apologize for and it just gets ridiculous.

Romance should be extremely meaningful, sentimental even; it helps to get creative and romance should always, always, always be appreciated, especially if you can tell your partner put a lot of thought and effort into a gesture. Shooting that down will emotionally scar your partner and chances are they'll never do anything like that for you again, not to mention fall into complete doubt over whether you actually care about them.

It's happened to me and it hurts.

I was married at a very young age and my husband and I had just moved into our own apartment. He was gone for work for about a month and I was pregnant with my oldest daughter. One of my close friends and I decided we would put a little welcome home gesture together for him the day he came back. Being the creative young people we were, we did some pretty elaborate things.

I had a fairly large mirror and wrote, "I love you," on it in purple nail polish, then set up some potpourri and candles so that the light would be reflected in the mirror. I wrote a poem for him on a poster board and stood it up behind the mirror and its candles and potpourri. I made a nice dinner for us, too, and set the table, also putting candles on it. Everything looked beautiful!

I left to go pick him up from work, excited to see him and show him how much I loved him. As we got back and went upstairs to our front door, I stopped him and said, "Wait here for just a minute so I can get your surprise ready."

I went in, lit the candles, and set the food out for us before asking for him to come in.

He barely even looked at the mirrored masterpiece set up in our living room.

"That's nice," he said.

I was crushed. I had spent hours of my time that day writing out a poem, decorating, cleaning, and cooking… for an unenthused, "That's nice." Of course then I began questioning why. Was my poem that bad? Was it too girly or lame? Was the food terrible?

Self-doubt settled in for me and the seed of resentment was planted in my mind for him. You can see how this would become a much bigger issue in the long run.

Last but not least, social time. It's a bonus if you have the same friends or eventually wind up being friends with the same people, but everyone needs their space to let loose with the guys or the girls and have fun without trying to live up to any expectations they may have unwittingly set up for themselves in their partner's eyes.

On top of that… you wouldn't want to hang around and ruin someone else's night when all they really wanted was a chance to get away and forget about an issue you're facing at that time, right? Venting and confiding in friends can give a fresh perspective on a problem, just like socializing without venting can give a person enough time to stop thinking about it for their subconscious to work out some ideas for solutions. Never underestimate the power of a guys' (or girls') night out.

The Third Pillar: Be Open to Possibilities

"The only limits to the possibilities in your life tomorrow are the buts you use today." –Les Brown

Being open to possibilities can be hard for people who have a certain idea of what they want or are absolutely opposed to getting to know people who don't fully "measure up." Now, I don't mean date every loser or user that's out there (done it more than too many times… not fun in the long run), but get to know people and decide based on their personality and your connection, whether you see it going further or not.

A lot of times this is kind of pointless to keep in mind if you still get infatuated easily because then your mind is pretty much made up as of first conversation (ah, to be young…). But, if you're thinking about getting back out there and want to approach it in the best, most constructive way possible, this section may be helpful.

If you have certain hang-ups about the opposite sex that make you judge people instantly, it might be time to examine those hang-ups a little bit. Mine was always height… If a man wasn't 6' or taller, I was instantly put off. I'm 5' 9" and have never been petite. Even as a skinny person, I'm not petite. So, naturally, I always loved it when a man could make me *feel* small.

For a while after I got braces, I had a huge issue with teeth. I still do to a point, but oral health concerns me way more than whether someone's teeth are "perfect" or not.

Don't lie; every single one of you reading this has some trait that you get caught up on (or used to, if you've already moved past it), maybe more than one. It's normal! But sometimes, getting past these traits that you think are so important can open doors you didn't even know existed before, which is why I'm writing this chapter in the first place.

If you meet someone and hit it off, do you immediately cut yourself off because of this one trait that you can't look past? Ouch! What if someone did that to you? "Oh, well she's not skinny enough so I won't even talk to her." Or, "He's got crooked teeth, so I can't talk to him."

Doesn't feel very nice, but also… what if that person ends up being the very person you need in your life and you just don't know it yet? May not know it for months or even years? What if you remain open and get to know this person, only to have them be an incredible friend for the rest of your life, or even just for the next ten years?

"Take your mind off the problems for a moment, and focus on the positive possibilities. Consider how very much you are able to do." –Ralph Marston

Just like a romantic relationship, a friendship is based on trust and open communication, just to name a few. If you see this person as only a friend, then say so! Don't lead them on. But if you're undecided, why let that hinder you from getting to know them better just because they have one or two traits that you consider to be flaws? Nobody's perfect, remember?

Another reason I bring up being open to possibilities is because the traditional way of meeting people just doesn't cut it anymore. Where people used to meet at restaurants, bars, and football games, people now meet online a lot more often. To drive this home, just look at all of the dating sites out there, not to mention all of the niche dating sites that focus on specific demographics: Black People Meet, Christian Mingle, dating sites for women who want to date wealthy men, dating sites for overweight women, and so on. It's crazy! There are just *so many* of them.

For people who are extremely busy or don't get out much, this is definitely a good way to meet people. Meeting online allows you to talk to people before actually meeting (which helps to determine whether someone is psychotic or not, but also how well you converse) in person.

Another bonus is that, no matter how bad a speller someone is, they usually text on their phones anyway. Texting is irritating to some people when everything is abbreviated (like me), but can still be dealt with. If you're comfortable enough with the person to give your number, then a phone call might be in order to see if you mesh that way.

Online dating can be daunting at first, but once you get a feel for it, you can learn to tell when someone is creepy or not just by reading how they write to you. Trust your instincts – we talked about trusting yourself in the first pillar, and it applies to online dating just as much as traditional dating.

Another thing to keep in mind is that the person you might be happiest with may or may not live nearby. What if your soul mate lives across the country or in Europe or Australia? Would you want to exclude them simply because they aren't local? It may not be comfortable for some people to do the long distance thing, but it can be done and done well, especially with the internet and technology being what it is today. You can Skype for free, and video chat comes pretty close to being around someone in person.

With all of that said, let's move on to the next pillar.

The Ten Pillars of a Happy Relationship
Jennifer-Crystal Johnson

The Fourth Pillar: Infatuation

"When you have seen as much of life as I have, you will not underestimate the power of obsessive love."
–J. K. Rowling

Oh, this little demon of a feeling can make people do some pretty crazy things in the name of love! The beauty of it is that if it's a mutual feeling, it can be a perfect foundation for a lasting, happy relationship. You know which feeling I'm talking about. Your heart races, stomach is filled with butterflies, you feel nervous and excited, and rejection can be a devastating thought that churns your stomach… or, in some cases, induces vomiting. Yikes!

You try to hide it but your entire being wants to profess your love for this person and shout it from the rooftops! You live, eat, drink, and breathe nothing but this person, this amazing individual whom you feel you cannot live without.

Three months later…. The kid gloves come off, "best behavior" becomes less pertinent, arguments are had, and that fluttering in your heart slows back down to its normal, steady beating. What happened?

Infatuation was mistaken for love too soon. The warm fuzzy feelings took over and skipped the part where you have to get to know, respect, trust, and love your partner. It's so easy to let infatuation sweep you off your feet – it feels so right! But you still have to maintain some semblance of control, otherwise the infatuation fizzles out and dies. What a pity! If properly nurtured and grown, it might have lasted. You know that saying about the flame that burns the brightest going out the fastest? That can definitely be applied here.

Infatuation feels powerful and intense. It can either be dangerous or it can be useful. The danger comes when you let fear take over and begin acting in ways that essentially send up red flags for the person you're infatuated with. That's not to say that you shouldn't follow your instincts – quite the contrary. However, if you are of the mind that your infatuation will fail or this person will end up leaving and these thoughts consume you, chances are that you're not ready for a lasting relationship because you haven't built a healthy relationship with yourself yet.

Infatuation can serve as a good foundation for a happy, romantic relationship if and only if both partners choose to put in the work required. From the infatuation, a friendship can be forged through communication, activities, and spending quality time together. For me personally, conversation is one of the most important aspects of a relationship. How am I supposed to be with someone if I can't have good conversations with them?

Through these conversations and being honest and respectful toward each other, a bond of friendship is formed. It's this friendship that creates a healthy transition from infatuation and feeling crazy to a relationship that has room to grow. There are several factors involved in nurturing the infatuation and making the transition to love.

- Developing a friendship
- Mutual respect
- Honesty
- Open communication
- Good conversations
- Compatible core values
- Selflessness
- Compromise
- Sacrifice

How many times have you seen an older couple still doing little things like holding hands and giving flowers? The way these veteran couples look at each other, you would almost think they were still in their honeymoon phase. Case in point – my parents. First marriage for both of them, married for over 25 years, and my dad still buys my mom flowers, they go out on dates, and they hang out together. The funny part is that they don't really have a whole lot of things in common aside from their core values. They just love each other and have supported one another through some pretty rough times. Those helped them to bond. And my dad still looks at my mom like she's the center of his universe. It is adorable! I bet they still get butterflies in their stomachs at times, too. My grandparents in Germany were the same way.

Maybe part of it is fate, sure. Maybe there are only a handful of people who could possibly be your "one." But no matter what you believe about true love, the fact remains that relationships require work, attention, and nurturing in order to succeed. They require knowing your own needs as well as the needs of your partner. They require an exchange of information about what can be done differently to grow the relationship and keep it healthy. They require self-control as far as your own actions are concerned. They require constructive problem-solving and compromise.

It's no surprise that 50% of marriages fail. That sounds like a lot of work! But if you begin with a mutual attraction and infatuation, both of you will be more likely to remain open to change, development, and the effort it takes to keep the relationship happy and strong.

The other 50% of marriages succeed, some of them very happily. These are the people to emulate and learn from – those who are still in love 10, 20, 30, or more years down the road.

It's the Little Things

When you think about the issues you have with someone in your past or present, what is usually the first thing that comes to mind (if it wasn't something seriously messed up like cheating or abuse)?

For many of us, it's the culmination of a bunch of little things that disappointed us and were either never addressed or never improved upon by our partners.

And if you really stretch yourself once all the anger and resentment has faded, what's the first thing that comes to mind in the spirit of appreciation of someone who severely messed up? Probably a little thing they did or used to do that was very touching, right?

I cannot stress to you how much of a difference the little things make, good or bad, especially if they're consistently displayed and used over the long haul. The little things are incredibly important.

> "Enjoy the little things, for one day you may look back and realize they were the big things." –Robert Brault

For example, someone I was with many years ago was verbally, sexually, and emotionally abusive toward me, but he had his moments of kindness. He is not an inherently evil or bad person, despite spousal rape, manipulation, coercion, a loaded gun in my face, constant accusations of cheating, and blaming me for "making" him carve the word PAIN into his own arm while I wasn't even in the room. Those things happened, sure… but I prefer to think of better things because I don't enjoy dwelling on the bad, especially now that it's been over for so long.

My favorite moment to recall when I start slipping into resentment (because I don't want to feel that at all – negative emotions are toxic to a good life) about this person: I remember a time when the hot water heater went out and I'd wanted to take a bubble bath to relax. He immediately jumped into action and started boiling pots of water in our largest pots so that I could take that bubble bath. How sweet is that? This is why I know he isn't a horrible person permanently or completely. I'd rather think of him doing little things like this for whomever he's with now than all of the messed up stuff he did to me.

Likewise, let's take a look at the other end of the spectrum. If your partner has a habit that is just absolutely disgusting and you ask him to stop or keep it away from other people, I believe it would behoove your partner to respect your wishes and do so because it's something small. I once was with someone who had a horrible habit of blowing his nose into the nearest shirt or dish towel. Yuck! Because guess who had to do that laundry? That would be me. This particular person continued to do this even after I brought it up and then, when my irritation built up and I got angry about it, he'd whine about being a failure and throw a pity party. Clearly not the way to solve a problem, right?

Both of those examples made a huge impact on my opinion on each of these people. And that's exactly what the little things do: they influence your perception of other people. And each person's perception, unless they figure out how to see beyond it, is their reality.

As an individual, wouldn't you like to be able to positively impact someone's perception of you with just a small change? I know I would. I'm not saying that you should go around changing who you are, but little habits, especially those that are either harmful, disgusting, or give a horrible first impression, are in need of changing anyway – not necessarily for your partner, but for yourself.

It isn't just that, though. These same little things that you do and see in your relationship with your partner have the ability to either make your relationship happier or utterly demolish it. Now, if you have the wherewithal and the self-awareness to maintain at least a somewhat objective point of view, in my opinion the responsibility to make changes falls on you, even if you feel like it's your partner's fault and they should be taught a lesson.

Why do I say this? Well, not everyone is self-aware, and not everyone even knows that self-awareness is a thing, and even if they do, they could be the type who denies everything because of their pride or ego. To make changes in a relationship, it takes one of the participants to make the first move. If no one makes the first move, well… the relationship will spiral downward and out of control.

If you are the person seeing the issues in the relationship, then you are the person with the power and responsibility to change things through example and leadership.

So, is Infatuation Good or Bad?

If you have a hard time maintaining self-control, it could easily be argued that infatuation is a bad thing and should be avoided. The truth is that it isn't black and white, and it isn't the same way for everyone. Infatuation, if given the proper nurturing, could very well transition into love.

> "There's a big difference between falling in love and being in love. There's a big difference between infatuation and falling in love." –Phil McGraw

My suggestion is to be aware of it. Know that your emotions, as much as they look like love, are merely chemical reactions in the brain. Also know that infatuation will fade; when it does, there needs to be something else there if you plan to maintain the relationship. The best thing that could be there is a newly developing friendship that can easily function as the foundation for true and lasting love.

If you feel that you wouldn't be able to keep these things in mind and function somewhat rationally while being infatuated, then I recommend avoiding that intense feeling if you can. It can definitely cause a lot of problems if you don't know how to handle it or are jumping into things too quickly.

The Fifth Pillar: Trust

"Trust is to human relationships what faith is to gospel living. It is the beginning place, the foundation upon which more can be built. Where trust is, love can flourish."
–Barbara Smith

This is a very sticky and uncomfortable topic for some people, especially those who have a hard time trusting anyone because of things that have happened to them in the past. Wouldn't it be nice if we were able to start fresh with the right person right away with no trust issues? It would be the perfect relationship, wouldn't it? Nope, still wrong. It could still flop while the couple with a sordid past ends up being happier together.

Each of us has our own unique set of life experiences to draw from and learn from, *not* to hold over an innocent person's head as a manipulation tactic or an excuse for our own questionable – sometimes even unacceptable – behavior.

"To be trusted is a greater compliment than being loved."
–George MacDonald

Having said that, here's a little secret: I have trust issues. Do I let them run my life? No way! Benefit of the doubt is something I'm pretty good at, though other, more cynical people are quick to point out failed relationships due to my being too trusting. Let me just say that I'd rather try whole-heartedly and fail than try half-heartedly and "succeed." Who has ever heard of "sort of" being in love? "Sure, I'm happy, I guess." What kind of life would that be? Better question: what kind of relationship would that be? A half-hearted one. That might be fine for some people, but I'm a dreamer and I dream big! I don't expect perfection, but I refuse to settle into a relationship just because it's convenient or seems like a good idea at the time. If my heart's not in it, I end it with an honest reason....

... Which brings us back to trust. In my experience, trust has a number of layers and infinite idiosyncrasies and characteristics depending on the people involved. The basics are usually there, though.

First, every individual has a specific amount of trust they will give right off the bat. This varies for everyone; my stance on it is to trust unless given a reason not to. Unfortunately, the reason not to could be something as petty as a friend telling me something specific about this person. The seed is planted, and any similar situations will prompt an immediate recollection of what my friend said. Is that fair? Probably not. Just because someone has made mistakes in the past doesn't mean they will repeat those mistakes. On the contrary; they might never do whatever it was again because they learned from their experience. That depends on the individual, though. Everyone handles things and solves problems in their own ways, and some people don't solve problems at all, opting instead to bury whatever the problem is and pretend it doesn't exist. Ah, the power of denial.

"Learning to trust is one of life's most difficult tasks."
–Isaac Watts

Obviously trust is a complex topic. In order to have a meaningful relationship – let's say the infatuation is there and you're in the honeymoon phase – the immediate trust should be nurtured and expanded on. Though everyone has their own perception of how to build trust, some things you can do to build it are fairly simple.

Keep your promises. This sounds like common sense, but is more easily forgotten than you might think. If it's a big deal to your partner and you forget, that sends the message that you don't place as much importance on their needs or wants as you probably should. Without conscious effort, this can be an easy and detrimental habit to fall into. Again, self-awareness comes into play here. If you make a promise, keep it. If you feel like you might forget, be honest about it – ask your partner to remind you closer to the time when you actually plan to make good on your promise.

Be yourself consistently. This can be difficult if you fall into the trap of trying to impress someone with things that aren't true. If you tell your partner you had a 3.5 GPA in college and turn around and tell his parents you had a 3.9, it's likely that your partner will wonder what else you're capable of lying about like that. Then they'll wonder if you're lying to them about anything, and trust is damaged.

Be supportive in the presence of others. What I mean here is that you should either stand up for your partner in a disagreement or handle it diplomatically before discussing things in private. If your partner is having a discussion with someone and you get pulled into it, diplomacy is best if you disagree with your partner. The last thing you want to do is create a feeling of conflict in the relationship by embarrassing your partner in front of others.

Avoid keeping secrets. If your partner has been hurt in the past, there will likely be some lingering trust issues to heal. This is especially true for people who have been cheated on. When this is a factor, being open and honest is extremely important for both partners and lessens the chances of a misunderstanding or an overreaction.

Confide in each other. When you share your opinions, your past experiences, your feelings, and your ideas, you help to open up the other person by doing so. Telling your partner about something that you don't share with everyone is a good way to extend an invitation to trust you in return because you have trusted them not to tell anyone what you shared.

Don't be judgmental. If your partner confides in you about a mistake they've made, stay supportive. Offer empathy and potential solutions, because if you laugh at them or make them feel dumb, the likelihood of them confiding in you again is lowered and trust in the relationship deteriorates. If you ever feel attacked after confiding something, let your partner know that you need to feel safe when sharing, and you feel attacked instead. They may not know that their reactions are breaking down trust.

Your flaws are lovable, too. When you open up and show someone your flaws, you give your partner the opportunity to love you for who you truly are. Even if you have insecurities about yourself, your partner may find those very things attractive. By opening up and being vulnerable with your partner, you're placing trust in them and vice versa. Remember, no one is perfect – and everyone prefers being loved for who they truly are as opposed to just on the surface.

Once the initial trust is nurtured and expanded on, another layer of trust has been earned and the process can be repeated. What happens if trust is not nurtured? It either sits there, stagnant (not likely) or is cracked or broken. A white lie, asking forgiveness instead of permission as an excuse to do something you know your partner wouldn't like (I'm sure everyone has heard this saying at some point), hiding a friendship with a member of the opposite sex – all of these seemingly little things can damage trust.

The best way to keep trust growing and building a stronger bond is through honesty. I know that personally, I would rather hear something I might not like from the mouth of my partner than find out three weeks later from a mutual friend or by some other means. If you mess up, admit it! It was a mistake, or an accident, or whatever. If you're honest about it, your trust might be a little damaged but not completely shattered. (This does not mean you can go out and make the same mistake five times and expect forgiveness because you told your partner each time. If you make the same mistake twice, trust will be fractured because you've already been forgiven once. This should be common sense.)

The thing to remember with honesty is to be honest in a tactful and kind way. Being up-front and honest is your best bet for developing a good sense of trust. You can literally see the bond between two people in love because they are very genuinely and kindly open with each other. This is shown through how they treat each other, their body language, and how they act when their partner isn't around to "police" them.

Honesty is still the best policy, especially if there's a chance – even just a remote chance – that your mistakes will come back to haunt you and fracture the trust you build with your partner.

"For every good reason there is to lie, there is a better reason to tell the truth." –Bo Bennett

Just to get down to some actionable and more tangible ways of building trust, let's look at some of the facets of honesty and building trust. There are many ways to be dishonest, and none of them involve much integrity. The most important aspect of being honest is to use tact and common sense. If you can be tactful when sharing your opinions with your partner, chances are the reception will be much better than if you're sarcastic, insulting, or express your opinions as facts, because they're not.

It's also important to remember that, just because something pops into your head doesn't mean you immediately have to go tell your partner all the details. For example, a scenario that can happen to anyone is having an erotic dream about someone other than your partner. Dreams and the subconscious are interesting because dreaming about this doesn't automatically mean you want to have an affair. It may mean something completely different. But is it really vital to tell your partner about it, or would you simply be appeasing your own guilt? Depending on your partner and the situation, some logic and thought should be applied here before making a decision to say something or not. By vocalizing the dream, you may be making a mountain out of a mole hill that could have resolved itself had you just kept your mouth shut.

Another typical example: "Does this dress make me look fat?"

Obviously you don't want to say yes to that, even if you do think it isn't the best dress on her. However, if it looks terrible and you go to an event where there are a lot of people, do you think she would appreciate being saved from that embarrassment, or being appeased and later hearing about what everyone else thought about her dress? I know that I would prefer knowing if I didn't look as good as I could and being spared all that embarrassment. I'd like to think that most other people would feel the same, as long as it was brought up in a tactful and kind way. Suggesting another dress that you know looks stunning is a good way to circumvent the situation. If she values your opinion (which should be a given in a healthy relationship), she'll take it into consideration and may even change just because you like the other dress better.

Being honest about friendships with the opposite sex is another good way to avoid breaking a trust that you are trying to build. Be up-front with your partner from the beginning. There will always be those people who are overly possessive and jealous, which I personally can't stand because it means they're too insecure to trust me or even themselves, but being honest about it and making sure your partner knows about the nature of these relationships is a good idea. Most people without a lot of insecurity and jealousy issues will understand and accept that if they have any friendships with the opposite sex then they will have to be okay with their partner having the same.

If you find that you've made a mistake or gotten yourself into a questionable situation, tell your partner right away. There's nothing worse than finding out through the grapevine that someone kissed your partner and they let it happen, which may or may not be the full story. At that point it's just hearsay, but you heard it from someone else and that alone is enough to make you lose trust in them.

Being honest is definitely not always easy, but if something is worth fighting for, then why try to weasel your way out of it in a dishonest manner?

The last thing I want to touch on in this chapter is being self-aware (there it is again!). I talked about this concept quite a bit in previous sections, but I feel it's worth mentioning again because I've witnessed how destructive a lack of self-awareness can be.

Self-awareness allows you to be honest with yourself and admit your own shortcomings, which is the most important part of being honest. If you lie to yourself, you'll have no problems lying to others. Aside from that, it makes you respect yourself more if you can trust that you'll do what's right, even if the mistake was your fault and fessing up might make you look bad for a short time. In the long run, you will have been honest about something that's difficult to be honest about, and that will stick with people, your partner included.

If someone brings forward a concern about you, your behavior, or your recent decisions, especially if they do so tactfully, then it's time to consider the possibility that you're doing things that are detrimental to you. I've had several experiences with this from both sides of the coin. Neither position is easy, especially if you have to bring up the same behaviors over and over or you have to hear how you're messing up over and over. But taking an honest look at yourself and seeing what's really going on is a good idea for your overall health and happiness.

I lost a very good friend over this very thing. For years, many in our close-knit group (myself included) tried to talk to her about her anger issues and let her know that she needed help. About a year before the friendship ended, every time I'd tell my kids that she'd be coming over for the weekend, they all responded with resounding disappointment and dread. "Aw, man!" they'd say, not looking forward to weekends that were supposed to be full of fun family time.

After an incident with her boyfriend's son getting a fat lip, I found out that she'd left marks on him before and that her anger had escalated into abusive behavior. I also found out that she had been lying not only to me, but to herself as well, perfecting the art of denial that she was doing anything wrong.

The whole situation made me very sad, especially once I realized that it would take a great deal more than my talking to her and writing her letters to make her realize that how she was behaving was wrong, pure and simple.

On the flip side, I've had friends approach me with issues in my own life and taken it personally at first, but once I got the whole story and sat down to talk with them about it, the friendship was that much better because the issues at hand were resolved.

If someone is concerned about you and has the decency to bring it up and let you know, then that means they sincerely care and know that you can be a better person.

I'd say that's a pretty loving thing to do, and important to pay attention to because if you don't respect the other person enough to take their opinions into consideration and sincerely try to better yourself, then they may decide you've become toxic. No one likes toxic people in their lives, and to be honest, these types of people usually have to be booted at some point. Some may disagree, and I've read and heard about ways to see around the toxicity, but saving yourself the drama of constantly having to deal with someone like this (an emotional vampire) is usually the easiest and best thing for you and your life. Even just backing off for a while and not subjecting yourself to them on a regular basis may help.

That brings us to the next pillar and how it ties in with all of the others.

The Sixth Pillar: Respect

♫"R-E-S-P-E-C-T, you know what it means to me!"♫

Actually you probably don't because you have your own idea of what respect looks like, but that's okay (and yes, I did just literally burst into song like my life is a musical!). Respect is a lot like trust; it has to be earned. I mean we all have a level of respect for people without them needing to earn it (just like trust), but that can be heightened or lowered within the first ten minutes of meeting someone. You may just not be on the same level as they are.

Mutual respect that meshes well is absolutely one of the most important aspects to a healthy, happy relationship. Without that level of respect, the relationship suffers. Although that suffering might be great for daytime TV ratings and sub-par talk shows, in our daily life we should nurture the respect we have for our partner.

Trust is largely dependent on the other person while respect is largely determined by your own perception of someone. That means, if you're involved with someone romantically, it falls on you to appreciate and respect the qualities you enjoy about that person. Now I'm not saying you should live in complete denial of someone's faults and blindly worship them – that's not healthy in any reality that I know of. The point is, though, that you can control how you choose to see people while they are generally just being themselves.

Any feeling fluctuates over time. Trust, respect, love… they all change based on the behaviors, words, and actions of both parties involved. Perceptions of people change and fluctuate as well. Being aware of this happening can help a great deal with creating and maintaining a happy relationship.

"One of the most sincere forms of respect is actually listening to what another has to say." –Bryant H. McGill

So how is respect lost? Naturally this will vary from one person to the next, but in general, respect can be lost if you perceive something about another individual that you don't have any respect for. This could be something from their past, something about how they speak, something about how they dress or present themselves, something about their hygiene habits, something about the way they act, or about a million other things, depending on how nitpicky you are.

I was extremely close with a couple who started out happy and ended up being at each other's throats almost constantly. The thing is that only one of them was doing the arguing at first; the other was "taking it" and trying to get out of the argument. The instigating party would find fault in nearly everything their partner did and complain about it, not just to them but also to everyone else, including me. It was like there was no possibility for conversation unless complaining and nagging was involved.

Meanwhile, some of the things that were complaints were small and almost petty, like making a huge issue out of the kids still being in pajamas on Saturdays when all they were doing was relaxing, anyway. It was a constant battle of months, and every time it happened, this person would literally fly off the handle and nag their partner for hours about it. I don't know about you, but if my kids and I decide to have a lazy day, I really don't care what they're wearing, as long as we hang out together and have fun.

Another common complaint was the way their partner spoke. Over time, this behavior drove this person crazy, even though nothing had changed from the time they first started dating. Somehow it became a flaw that was completely unacceptable, even though it wasn't any different from before.

While one person was laser-focused on the negative, the other was trying desperately to maintain a positive perception of the complainer, and still doing things like getting up with the kids, letting the other person go out and being the babysitter, and cleaning the house. It was a very interesting dynamic to see because it was so unbalanced, and it was making the entire family miserable.

The funny part is that your partner was doing these things all along; people don't change overnight and they usually have the same kinds of little habits for years. Although you may not have *seen* those habits before moving in together, they had at least some of them. You can choose to accept them, confront them, or try to ignore them, but no matter which way you choose, it is your perception of these habits that lowers your respect for your partner. Each person has their own ideas about what is acceptable and what isn't. Maybe the habits that you absolutely despise or get on your nerves are what your partner grew up with and thinks are normal?

When all is said and done, it boils down to mutual respect for each other *and* for the relationship itself. If your partner does something that drives you nuts, talk about it. Let them know how you feel. Maybe it's a disgusting habit or something you feel embarrassed about when in public with them. The best way to solve respect issues is to first make your partner aware – tactfully, please – of their habits that bug you. They probably don't even know it bothers you so much (after all, no one is a mind reader). Because a relationship needs compromises, your partner can begin trying to break whatever habit or habits you don't like. The same should be done in reverse; if your partner finds some of your habits disruptive, try your best to compromise. If compromise can't be reached, hopefully the act of communicating and then trying raised both partners' respect levels on principle. This should allow for acceptance of the habits without too much loss of mutual respect.

Please note that this will never work if it's one-sided. If there's something fairly big that you feel your partner needs to change, it becomes more difficult. One thing to keep in mind is that positive reinforcement will always trump punishment or complaining and nagging.

For most of us, it's usually the little things that add up to make the biggest difference positively or negatively. Completely ignoring it when your partner brings something up that bothers them is a sure fire way to drag their respect for you through the mud… And vice versa.

Some Thoughts on Positive Reinforcement

Positive reinforcement is used in raising children, training pets, and many other areas of life. Why not apply it to relationships? Nagging your partner to death isn't very likely to achieve the results you want; as a matter of fact, a lot of people respond by either ignoring the nagging or rebelling against it even more.

So how do you implement positive reinforcement?

If your partner does something you don't like, ignore it. When they do what you would prefer them to in place of the undesirable habit, reward them with praise, gratitude, or a kiss – or all of the above. Simple, right?

For example, if your partner throws their dirty laundry on the bedroom floor instead of in the hamper, ignore it. Don't pick it up, don't touch it, but don't nag about it, either. Just simply ignore it. You could even simply say, "Well, I'm not washing anything that isn't put in the hamper because that's my signifier to know that it needs to be washed."

If they do put their clothes in the hamper, say thank you or praise them for it. Give them a big hug and a kiss. Not only will the floor be cleaner, but their laundry will actually get washed. Clean clothes are good!

After a few times, the behavior should start to improve. The other bonus is that, with less nagging in the home, there will be less arguments and tension.

There's another little tidbit I want to talk about in this chapter along the same lines and that is learning to pick your battles.

Picking your battles involves learning how to let go of things that irritate you that are petty or unimportant. Learning to let go of some of these little habits or traits involves a lot of internal work, just like most of the topics in this book. And really, the only way to get truly good at any of this is to put it into practice on a daily basis.

I firmly believe that someone who is habitually a nagger has no ability to let go of things that are unimportant. No matter what you do or how much you try to make them happy, they will always, always, *always* find something to nag or complain about. I can tell you from personal experience that this is absolutely zero fun and the nagger ends up being really difficult to care about because they make everyone around them miserable.

> "He just irritates me so much with his habits. It's like everything I say just goes in one ear and out the other," she confided in me. I nodded my head in agreement, understanding that it can be frustrating.

> "Maybe you should try approaching it in another way," I suggested, hoping to end this repeat of the same conversation we'd had a million times.

> With a know-it-all look on her face, she replied, "I've tried everything. Nothing works. He just doesn't get it."

"Well, then you have to ask yourself whether it's worth it to get so worked up about these little things. In the big picture, does it really matter if the kids are in PJs on the weekend or that he doesn't speak perfectly?"

"It's just frustrating and messes with my OCD," she replied.

My only thought at that point was that OCD was being used as an excuse for negative and toxic behavior, and I knew that she had not, in fact, tried *everything*. I had a front row seat to the deterioration of this relationship between two people I cared about, and nothing was being done to constructively solve any problems. I was sick of talking about it and making the same suggestions; she was sick of "having to" nag all the time, and her partner and the kids were sick of the constant fighting.

One way to solve this issue if you or your partner have a tendency to complain is to keep a gratitude journal. At the end of every day, sit down and write a small list of three things that your partner did that day that you feel grateful for. Once you've both written this down, sit and share it with each other. The best way to do so is to sit facing each other and get to a point of openness in your thoughts and mood.

Getting yourself into an attitude of gratitude will make a big difference in the way you perceive everything in your life, and if you make it a point to do this for 30 days, you will be well on your way to seeing things more positively. That in turn will lead to finding less things to complain about. Instead, you'll be forming the habit of finding things to be grateful for and hopefully realize how damaging it is to complain all the time. I have seen this method recommended a number of times in various contexts including business and personal development, and simply having that attitude of gratitude is a good way to get your life to the point where you want it to be.

In a relationship, if your partner does something for you or goes out of his or her way to make your life easier, it is extremely important to say thank you, too. Make sure that this phrase becomes a part of your daily life.

It is absolutely amazing to me how much being grateful for what you have can bring you in terms of happiness. Again, it involves a lot of internal work, but that's how we become the best version of ourselves that we can be!

What is Internal Work?

I've mentioned internal work a lot in this book already, so I thought it might be good to give you a better idea of what I mean when I say this. Internal work is work you do within your own mind, thoughts, and personality. For example, when you try to break or form a habit. Habit replacement can work here, too, but let's just say you have a habit of worrying about money. When you focus on how badly you need more money as opposed to focusing on solutions you can implement now to stretch the money you do have, that puts added strain on you and decreases your happiness because you worry a lot about it.

It becomes difficult when you have debt collectors calling you or other debt that needs to be taken care of. Where money is concerned, I want to share a little story. And yes, I was lucky to have the help of my parents, but the stress and anxiety was still present until I had an epiphany.

> My phone rang. I looked at it to see a private number calling. *Great,* I thought. *What is it this time?*
>
> "Yes, I'm calling about a debt you owe to ABC company in the amount of $800. Is there any way you can make a partial payment for that amount today?"

"No, it hasn't changed since yesterday… or the day before… or the day before."

"Well, ma'am, it's already in collections and will be on your credit for a long time unless it's taken care of today." My blood began to boil.

"Why don't you call my ex-husband who tried to kill me and make him pay child support? You're obviously way better at collecting money than the state is!" (Can you tell I was still very bitter at this time?)

"I don't need to know about that, ma'am."

I hung up the phone and started to cry. How in the world was I supposed to pay that off? I had no job, no money, two kids, and luckily enough a free place to stay… for now. Something had to change.

Then it hit me. I was giving all of this energy to my worries and exhausting myself, which wasn't helping my productivity or motivation at all.

There's absolutely nothing I can do about that debt right now. It's out of my control how often they call me and stress me out, but it's well within my control to choose which calls I actually pick up. I choose to let go of this worry until I can take care of it. It's time to focus on what I can do to better my life and the rest will fall into place.

That realization got me on a better track toward being happy, simply because I chose to stop focusing on the negative. I began trying to focus on the positive and enrolled in college, applied for state assistance to help out, and almost immediately, things began to improve. It was almost like my attitude changed everything.

I recommend trying it; the way you choose to look at things and feel about things is what I call internal work, because it must take place within your own mind and feelings. No one can accomplish this but you. Why not *choose* a happier life today?

"Everything can be taken from a man but one thing: the last of human freedoms – to choose one's attitude in any given set of circumstances, to choose one's own way."
–Viktor E. Frankl

The Seventh Pillar: Communication

What good is talking about what bothers you if the issues that need solving go in one ear and out the other? Obviously knowing how to communicate and practicing *active listening* are important parts to a happy relationship. People want to be heard and hope that their partners respect them enough to consider and make a note of what should be worked toward to continue growing and nurturing the relationship. Communication also has to do with the different love styles people have, as feeling loved plays a huge role in how issues are brought up and whether they end up being solved or not.

> "Any problem, big or small, within a family, always seems to start with bad communication. Someone isn't listening."
> –Emma Thompson

On average, we only actually hear between 25% to 50% of what someone tells us, and vice versa. Active listening is the practice of consciously focusing on what someone else is saying and clearly hearing their message, while passive listening is basically doing the bare minimum to hear another person. Most of us tend to only sort of listen and form counter arguments as we listen, or we get distracted by something else or even our own thoughts. One tip to be a better listener is to mentally repeat what someone has told you to yourself to improve retention of the message.

Another way to make sure you stay focused and that will help the person speaking to you feel like you're listening is to occasionally nod, recap their message, or say, "uh-huh," as they're speaking to you. These little things remind you to stay focused on what they're saying as well as reassuring the other person that you are, in fact, listening.

Let's face it… there's nothing more irritating than talking to someone and feeling like it's pointless to do so because they're not looking at you, not paying attention, or just simply not getting it. "Hello, wall... nice to meet you!"

How can you improve your active listening skills? Here are some basic tips to help you become a better listener.

1. Pay Attention
Look at the person speaking; make and maintain eye contact. Non-verbal communication is also important, so pay attention to their body language. Don't try to form a response while they're speaking or get distracted by other thoughts, conversations, or environmental stimuli.

2. Provide Appropriate Responses
When you practice active listening, you're showing the person respect. Your replies to what they say should also be respectful, open, and presented in a constructive way. The golden rule applies: treat the person as you would want them to treat you.

3. Be Aware of Your Body Language
It's important to show the speaker that you're listening. Nod, smile, and give verbal acknowledgment that you're paying attention. Make sure your body language remains open and inviting to encourage them to keep going.

4. Confirm Your Understanding
We all have filters and are programmed to make snap judgments no matter how hard we try not to. Because of this, it's important to make sure you're getting the point the speaker is trying to make. We also tend to have emotional responses to certain things being said. Try not to let this take over; instead, periodically paraphrase what the speaker has said and ask questions if you feel you aren't getting it completely. If you find yourself getting angry at something they said, double-check what they meant; it could be that their words came out differently than what they meant them to, which happens to the best of us!

5. Don't Judge

We often make snap judgments or get defensive about something someone says before they've even finished what they're saying. Make an active effort to listen to their complete thought. Interrupting just leads to frustration and usually to an argument. Make sure you ask questions and keep in mind that everyone is entitled to their own opinion.

We've all heard that communication plays an important role in relationships. It also plays an important role in friendships, business, leadership, and every other aspect of life that has anything to do with people. Unless you're a hermit living off on some mountain without electricity, running water, or a need for the grocery store, then some of these skills are definitely necessary.

Knowing how to communicate with people is absolutely essential to living. As an example, imagine you're a tourist in another country. How would you communicate that you're hungry, thirsty, or need a restroom? Most people try to learn the language of the country they're visiting specifically so they can get what they need when they need it.

"The most important thing in communication is hearing what isn't said." –Peter Drucker

Unfortunately, when it comes to relationships, simply knowing the same language as your partner doesn't mean you have good communication skills. Simply being able to talk and use words doesn't make you a good communicator. In a relationship, you also have to keep in mind *how* you communicate; what tone of voice are you using? How's your body language? Are you sounding accusatory or condescending (even if you're not trying to)? Is there a reason your partner might perceive you sounding like you're nagging even if you're not trying to? How are your conversations? Do you each give and take in somewhat equal proportions or is one person doing all the talking? Does one of you have a one-track mind and keep bringing the conversation back to the same topic, even if that topic has been closed? Do your discussions about issues in life or the relationship lead to solutions or just more problems or fighting? Does one of you sound cruel or callous because you're trying to be blunt and straight forward? Is the other too sensitive to handle that kind of honesty? If that same kind of honesty is used by the other person, do you get offended or your feelings hurt?

Obviously there are a million and one things that can go horribly wrong when you're communicating with someone. What makes communication in a romantic relationship so difficult is that the relationship is so emotionally charged that it can backfire. You've hung all of your hopes on this one person, this one relationship, and when you begin to see past the exterior "perfection" you've pinned on the one you love, your hope begins to crumble a little bit. If they seem unresponsive to requests you make for compromise or change in the day-to-day routine and habits, your hope cracks even more.

So if all of this can go wrong in trying to communicate with your partner, how in the world are you supposed to communicate with your partner?!

"To effectively communicate, we must realize that we are all different in the way we perceive the world and use this understanding as a guide to our communication with others."
–Tony Robbins

The short answer is to communicate respectfully and tactfully. If something is bugging your partner, you have to listen to what the problem is, acknowledge the part you play in said problem calmly, then discuss possible solutions to the problem. You should both also keep in mind that the solution – or the problem, either one – probably won't be easy or completely comfortable for either one or both of you to discuss, let alone solve. The way you communicate plays a huge role in whether the relationship will last or die out.

People are in relationships because they want to feel loved.

Let's read that one more time: People are in relationships because they want to feel loved. What many people don't realize is that this doesn't *just happen*. It can be practiced and developed.

There was a time when I felt completely isolated from people; like I was giving and giving and not receiving what I needed in return. I often felt taken advantage of and alone, even if I was around people who cared about me. It took a while, but I eventually realized that a big part of the reason why I felt like this was simply because of the way I thought about and perceived others' words and actions.

When making myself available to others, my expectation was that they would do the same for me. Because that expectation was there, I had an ulterior motive that tainted my relationship with that person, and if I needed someone to lean on and couldn't reach out for whatever reason, the disappointment was that much more severe because my expectation wasn't met.

I was telling myself that people don't care, and this was manifesting itself in my life because I gave energy and emotional power to that thought.

> "The game of life is a game of boomerangs. Our thoughts, deeds, and words return to us sooner or later with astounding accuracy." –Florence Scovel Shinn

When you begin to really open up and allow yourself to be vulnerable, magical things can happen. Being present in your conversations and situations as well as feeling appreciative of people's time and attention can work wonders for your ability to feel loved. We previously covered fear and how we speak to ourselves; this falls into the same category.

Some tips for feeling more loved:

- Be present in the moment and with those you're spending time with.
- Seek out honest, open, and reciprocal conversations.
- Avoid telling yourself negative things about love. Instead, know and believe that there is plenty of love in the world and you deserve it, too; it's on its way to you.
- Value and cherish your relationships… all of them. Don't focus on what's missing; instead, focus on those people who are already in your life and who care deeply about you.
- Give the kind of love you want to receive.
- Notice and appreciate little things people do for you and say to you. Be sure to say thank you and give praise and credit where it is due.
- Remember to love and appreciate yourself!

Now that you know a little more about letting yourself feel loved, how do you help make sure your partner feels loved? How does your partner make sure you feel loved? Does this just magically happen or is there more to it than that?

When you get a divorce and children are involved, the court orders you to take a parenting class. One of the parenting classes I took was incredibly informative, not just about parenting or relationships, but about some of the inner workings of people within their relationships. One of the things that has stuck in my mind throughout the years is the different styles of love people have. Everyone has a unique need that they need met in order to feel loved.

I want to briefly touch on these different love styles to help you get a better handle on why communicating has so many pitfalls. It's also a good idea to sit down and figure out what love style fits you and your partner best so you can consciously become aware of what you need to do to help your partner feel loved, and vice versa.

The love styles are as follows: physical, meaning that you feel love through touch, kissing, sex, hugging, and so on. Verbal, meaning that you feel love when you hear someone say that they love you; the words are enough for you to feel that you are loved. Material, meaning that you feel loved when you receive gifts from your partner or they take you out to dinner. Active, meaning that you feel loved when someone does things for you such as chores around the house or a massage when you're stressed out or overwhelmed.

Obviously most people are a combination of these; for example, I feel loved when someone does things for me, like mopping the kitchen or vacuuming, because that means I don't have to do it and relieves some pressure from me and my daily list of tasks, which can often be overwhelming. However, I also feel loved through getting hugs and being told that someone loves me. I feel loved through gifts, too, although that one is a bit more awkward for me personally. I don't generally like getting "stuff" as a main form of someone showing me they love me. Buying something is easy; putting in effort to help around the house is more difficult and I interpret that as a stronger love than just running to the store to get me something I may or may not even like or get any use from. That's just how I perceive love.

People are all different in how they handle things, too. Some people stand by their word to a fault – their word is literally their bond and they will not break it no matter what. I'm a little bit like this and try not to make promises or commitments if there's a chance I won't be able to keep them. Instead of making a promise and then letting someone down, I tend to be a little wishy-washy in my response and say something like, "I'll see what's going on and if I can do it or not." Though some people will still get offended if I end up not being able to make plans, most of the time this is a good way to keep things healthy and positive in the relationship, whether it's a friendship or a romantic relationship.

Other people are very quiet about their problems, can't stand confrontation, and hope the issues go away on their own. They typically do nothing and try to ignore their problems until they go away. This is a very dangerous path to walk on because things build up and build up until the pressure within them is too much and they eventually blow up in anger toward their partner and all of his or her shortcomings. Unfortunately, by the time the blowup happens, this person's sense of respect for the other has all but vanished and the feeling of being fed up outweighs – or at least feels like it outweighs – the love and caring that was once the focal point.

This actually happened to me with a romantic relationship before. Instead of focusing on the good aspects of our relationship, I focused on the bad aspects and let those tarnish my view of the other person. However, I was not very comfortable with bringing up problems, and so they festered there and became bigger and bigger. By the time I brought up what I felt was wrong, I was so irritated and angry about it that it turned into a massive and ongoing argument. Had I brought it up calmly with a focus on solutions, things would have been very different.

If you're lucky, both of you will recognize when there's a problem and seek counseling or make up your minds to try different ways of communicating. When you're angry with your partner or are having some kind of problem, remember the love you feel for your significant other. Sit face-to-face, hold hands, and remember the love. While sitting, both of you should take a few deep breaths and calm down! Then state what issue you're having and allow your partner to respond.

It helps to begin this kind of communication by listing three things about your partner that you're grateful for that day. By exchanging feelings of appreciation and gratitude, you put your mind and body into a calm state, which makes solving problems a hundred times easier. It also makes talking about problems much easier, as there is less of a chance that either person will blow up at the other or start yelling.

When you're face-to-face and touching, it suddenly becomes difficult to start yelling and screaming at your partner. You're right there in front of each other, not walking around doing something else while complaining at them or sounding angry. You'd be amazed to see how much difference that simple practice makes in both of your problem-solving abilities. Think about it: instead of being distracted with chores or other activities, you're forcing yourself to give your full attention to the relationship for a little while. You're also within whispering distance of each other, and this encourages closeness and conversational intimacy.

There is a Hindu love story that poses the question, "Why do we shout in anger?" It goes on to state that the closest hearts are so close that they don't even need to whisper to communicate anymore; all they need to do is look at each other. This is a beautiful example of how closeness can make us more open, comfortable, and constructive in dealing with life and all of its stress and problems.

Sitting face-to-face also cuts down on denial, which I'm sure everyone knows is a major setback when trying to find solutions to any problem. Those who live in denial will have a more difficult time acknowledging that they've done something wrong. This can easily cause frustration and resentment to build.

I spoke earlier about self-awareness and taking responsibility for your own actions and words; this is the way to move past the urge to deny everything and get defensive. Taking responsibility for yourself offers a profound feeling of freedom and peace once it's put into practice, a feeling that many don't know will exist by doing so. Denial is a fear-based response, and moving past that habit can ultimately make your life and relationships much happier.

For more about sitting down to face each other when communicating and how it can help you with your relationship, check out the book *Do You Want to Drive or Do You Want to Bitch?* by Sheldon Wayne Moss. I worked on editing this book and highly recommend that you read it if you want to have a long-lasting, happy relationship.

Communication is about sharing and solving problems; communicating with your significant other should be loving and respectful – and productive! You'd be able to go to your best friend with an issue and solve it with them, right? Why not with your partner? That's who you're in love with, and that kind of love should be based on a solid friendship. Doesn't that relationship deserve the best possible communication and problem-solving for that very reason?

"Take advantage of every opportunity to practice your communication skills so that when important occasions arise, you will have the gift, the style, the sharpness, the clarity, and the emotions to affect other people."
–Jim Rohn

The Eighth Pillar: Mutual Growth

"Our chief want is someone who will inspire us to be what we
know we could be."
–Ralph Waldo Emerson

This chapter has to do with growing together and inspiring each
other to do better things with your lives and continuously move
forward. Embracing positive change – or even change that doesn't
seem positive at first – is a wonderful quality to develop that will
make life as a whole easier. The point of being with someone is to
share life – if you're still or stuck for too long, life becomes boring
and just about surviving as opposed to actually living.

Life is a wonderful thing! Enjoying the ride, growing with your
partner, and mutually inspiring one another is an excellent way to
ensure that neither one of you get bored nor stuck in a rut. Of
course this takes some effort, but most aspects of a happy
relationship take effort. The point is to have positive habits
instead of negative ones, and a great deal of developing those
positive habits happens while you're working on your relationship
consciously.

So how can couples ensure that they are growing together? What
does that even mean? I don't believe it means doing the same
things and advancing at exactly the same pace – you are still
individuals, after all. It's more like accepting when your partner
does something new and knowing that he or she will also accept
when you do something new. It also means being supportive in
whatever endeavors each person undertakes. Going back to
school is a really excellent example, and one that I will use
throughout this chapter.

"Your life does not get better by chance, it gets better by
change." –Jim Rohn

Change is part of life. Some people thrive on it while others fear it; some people accept it – even enjoy it – while others feel like their lives are turned upside down by it. Change can be good or bad, that's true, but in order to fully enjoy life as a whole as well as your relationships, it's paramount to accept that things change and evolve over time no matter what your attitude toward that is.

I've personally always thrived on change because I grew up in a military family. We stayed in one place no longer than three years until I got to eighth grade, and at that point, I started doing crazy stuff like chopping off my hair when I got restless. I couldn't stand when things *didn't* change! It was an interesting adjustment for me to stay still. Back then, that need for change wasn't necessarily all good, but now, as an adult, I feel my upbringing served me well because if things change, I handle it fairly well and am able to deal with what's going on and continue moving forward. I also know that, no matter how stable you are in life, things will change sooner or later. It's the way these changes are perceived and handled that make them good or bad.

"If we don't change, we don't grow. If we don't grow, we aren't really living." –Gail Sheehy

Imagine that a man and a woman have been together for three years and they've hit a stalemate in their relationship, and thus their mutual life. The woman is bored out of her mind and the man is busy with his routine and kind of sleepwalking through day-to-day tasks and responsibilities. If the woman doesn't sit down with her partner to discuss her boredom, what do you think could happen? All kinds of craziness. She could go start getting tattoos and piercings, change her wardrobe, chop off her hair, dye her hair, have an affair, or even leave her partner. If no effort is made to communicate about this issue, there will be no mutually beneficial solution.

Any time change is involved, it tends to make people nervous. Change can be difficult. It can be intimidating. It can be awkward.

If one person wants more out of life while the other is comfortable where they are, this can become a conflict.

As an example of a negative conflict about it versus a positive conversation about it, let's see how things would look if he absolutely didn't like change and liked being where they are.

"Honey… I feel like we're stuck in a rut," she might say.

"Why do you say that?" He begins to get a little nervous.

"Because we just do the same thing every day and I feel as though we're not going anywhere. Like a hamster in a wheel, we're running in place."

"Well, I certainly don't feel like I'm not going anywhere," he says, getting a little agitated. "I work all the time and am hoping to get a promotion. We go out and do things with the kids. It's not like it's exactly the same every day."

"I just feel like I should be doing more with my life," she says, already regretting her decision to bring it up.

"What, being a wife and mother isn't enough?" he asks. "Maybe you should go and get a job, then," he adds scornfully. "That would certainly help *me* out, since you're obviously getting bored staying at home with the kids."

"I was actually thinking about going back to school," she retorts. "And it isn't because being a wife and mother isn't enough for me. It's simply because I'd like to have applicable knowledge."

"Fine, do what you want. As long as it doesn't interfere with my job, it's whatever." He storms off, intimidated by her desire to learn and afraid of losing her to positive change.

That conversation didn't sound very nice. It actually reminds me of how my ex-husband might've reacted to the notion of his wife going back to school. His need for control and fear of change would have taken over, not to mention that he would've been jealous, like he was when my first book was published.

Fortunately, not everyone has those issues that run their lives, and the conversation could look something more like this:

"Honey... I feel like we're stuck in a rut," she might say.

"Why do you say that?" He begins to get slightly nervous.

"Because we just do the same thing every day and I feel as though we're not going anywhere. Like a hamster in a wheel, we're running in place."

"So what do you think we should do about that?" He asks, wondering what part he'll have to play in this upcoming endeavor.

"I think I'd like to go back to school," she replies, getting excited. He can tell she's already done her research on the topic and has her hopes hung on attending college.

"But I like things the way they are... what would you going to college look like for our life as a whole?"

She takes the opportunity to explain her options to him and talk about what her area of study will be. She mentions that she can still be home with the kids and attend college classes online. He breathes a sigh of relief at that idea, but also knows he'll have to do more to help around the house when she's studying or doing homework.

He decides it's worth it. To see her this excited and passionate about something again makes him realize that they'd both gotten too caught up in the daily routine of things and need to spice up their lives a little.

In a perfect world, that's how the conversation would go… in reality, the potential for it to go similarly is definitely there. Maybe – just maybe – he would show her support, kindness, and encouragement to follow her dreams and better herself. Maybe her desire to do this would inspire him to do more, too. It could go either way; it could be he who wants to go back to school… but the best way to find out would be to communicate in a positive way.

"Progress is impossible without change, and those who cannot change their minds cannot change anything."
–George Bernard Shaw

To truly have a happy, lasting relationship, the committed individuals have to grow, learn, and change together. If one changes and the other falls behind, they hit an awkward point in their relationship. Maybe one of them is more driven to be successful than the other and their ambitions are on two completely different levels. Would one support the other's increasing drive and ambition? Would the other in turn continue to respect their partner even though their levels of ambition are far apart? That would depend on the individuals, but as you can see, there are a lot of factors that could be considered.

No matter what the individual factors might be, one thing is constant. If you and your partner don't learn and grow together or show support for the other's growth, one will feel inferior or left behind while the other might feel guilty or pity their partner, or even lose respect for their partner. That can change the dynamic of the relationship as a whole. To help prevent this from happening, both should keep communication open and discuss the things that interest and inspire them. So what if one partner isn't as ambitious as the other? Maybe that just means it's time to take up a hobby or learn something new. It could even mean going back to a hobby you treasured as a child.

Things will *never* always stay the same. Everything is in motion on a constant basis, if you think about it. We grow the most in our sleep. Our hair grows constantly. The earth is traveling at something like 36,000 miles per hour and we can't feel it. Our hearts are always beating, blood always pumping through our veins. Nothing is perfectly still. The average person has between 12,000 and 70,000 thoughts per day, depending on your sources. Neurons in the brain are firing, constant communication, constant motion, constant energy. On an atomic level, we *are* energy.

Life moves pretty quickly, too, especially in our age of instantly loading web pages and instant communication. We watch movies with the click of a mouse, information is being uploaded and downloaded constantly, we place orders and have food or coffee in hand within minutes, and we share our lives in status updates and 140-character tweets... is it any wonder that relationships and the people in them change almost constantly? Is it any wonder that people have less patience now?

I used to ponder this when I would write poetry in a corner booth at Denny's. I would begin by writing whatever popped into my head, whether it was "good" writing or not. I didn't worry about that. My goal was to capture a moment; this moment would then be eternally documented on a page in one of my journals, and I sincerely believed that I would never be that same exact version of myself again. The moment passed... the time cannot be taken back... and I was already someone else again, a new version of myself just another moment later, capturing the new moment before it passed... or trying to, anyway.

"As the birth and death
And decay of a moment
Rips everything apart
And puts it back together

Within a single second,
There is nothing left
Until later but the bliss
Of the birth and death
And decay of that moment."
—Jennifer-Crystal Johnson
(From journal #2, *Mosaic*)

Because we love the person we're with, it's important to support them and accept when they seek change. This has to go both ways. If one person is attending college but the other doesn't support them in it, grades will suffer and the enjoyment of the experience is diminished for the person attending college. There cannot be any double-standards here. That isn't healthy in a relationship.

Mutual growth means helping one another and doing whatever it takes to support and encourage the one you love. If they feel supported and encouraged, like they have someone positive in their corner, they will do much better with their endeavors than if they feel like they are in it alone.

I once knew a couple where he went to college but she was constantly criticizing and making negative comments about his grades. She was a stay at home mom to their kids, yet when it came time for him to do homework, she refused to help with the children because she felt she had played her part while he was in class. This obviously led to his grades suffering and his entire college career was affected by her lack of support in his endeavor. When it came time for her to return to school, he was expected to handle everything else while she was in class as well as while she was doing her work at home. To top it all off, she decided to go to the bar and leave him home with the kids several times a week; a complete double-standard as far as the relationship as a whole was concerned.

This example makes me think of one word: balance (the next pillar). It isn't just up to one person to do the work involved in maintaining a happy relationship. It's the responsibility of both people. This responsibility includes supporting one another, encouraging one another, and accepting when one person is making progress and the other isn't *without* taking on an attitude of superiority or inferiority. Each person must contribute to the relationship as a whole if it is expected to work long-term.

"If you change the way you look at things, the things you look at change." –Wayne Dyer

Unfortunately, this is not a skill most people are born with. It is a skill they learn over time, sometimes through years of "failed" relationships. However, once this supportive attitude is in place, the relationship can withstand many hardships, trials, and tribulations.

Being a part of each other's lives in a relationship is the whole point of the relationship, isn't it? So if your partner does something special, accomplishes a goal, or has a bad day, all of this should be shared, acknowledged, and appreciated. Life is change and forward motion; if your partner gets stuck, you can either help them out by supporting them or leave them behind. I suppose it all depends on how much you love them… and how much they love you in return.

The Ninth Pillar: Balance

"Happiness is not a matter of intensity but of balance, order, rhythm, and harmony." –Thomas Merton

You have nothing if you don't have balance. I mentioned this earlier and it is true beyond any doubt for me, based on what I've seen in my life as well as in others'.

Sometimes people get stuck in the notion that someone is out there who will make them happy. Someone will "complete" them.

The last time I checked, one plus one still equals two.

Having said that, here's the issue: when you go into life expecting someone else to take charge of *your* happiness, you're doing several things. One, you're putting a lot of pressure on that person to fill your "happiness cup" because you can't generate your own happiness. Two, you're offsetting the balance of what real happiness is. Three, you're messing up the balance of what a happy relationship can be!

"The Constitution only gives people the right to pursue happiness. You have to catch it yourself."
–Benjamin Franklin

If there are two people in a relationship, the goal is to be happy *together*, right? Happy, functional partners. A partnership, an agreement, but filled with love, affection, and maybe even children. If the goal is to be happy, then why is it that we often see people completely angry and ready to quit after two years, three years, or five years?

It's because of frustration. Frustration with life, frustration with situations or circumstances, frustration with money, frustration with your partner's way of dealing with things being different from your own… frustration. That pretty much sums up why I've seen most relationships end, including my own. What makes it worse is that you can never *force* your partner to listen to you or see things your way. You can't force understanding. You're so irritated and fed up that you can't talk to them without undertones of aggravation, but they will immediately sense that and assume you're nagging or bitching at them. No matter how hard you consciously try to sound nicer, you haven't dealt with the underlying issues on your own so your partner will only see you trying to hide your irritation.

As an example of how this frustration can build up and become overwhelming, let me tell you about a personal experience.

Before moving in together, my ex and I had to sit down to lay out some ground rules because he tended to be extremely messy and my son was only a toddler at that point. Things had to be somewhat clean around the house because this little boy got into everything!

Not only that, but the bills had to be paid. I didn't make very much money and neither did he, so we split everything in half. It was understood that, if I needed to work, he would need to help with the kids. He had his own office with a lock on the door, so the kids weren't an issue for him when he needed to get some work done.

It turned out that I was paying the majority of the bills and, if he were to get a job, I would have to drive him as he had no car or driver's license. So I told him he would simply need to take over more of the housework and watch the kids.

This worked alright for a few months, but before long, he was sleeping in until noon, disappearing into the garage to smoke cigarettes for about three hours, and then finally showing his face to help me out. Meanwhile, I had been trying to work for the entire day with a toddler constantly needing something, the other kids coming home from school, and my productivity being slowed down to a snail's pace.

I tried to bring it up to him calmly, but he didn't handle it very well. Instead of trying to make things better, he would immediately fall into pity-party mode and start crying, saying he's sorry he failed me, and essentially having an emotional breakdown. This man could not handle any kind of criticism, no matter how tactfully a problem was presented.

By the time another year had gone by, I was completely fed up. I was exhausted; tired of feeling like I had to do everything, tired of feeling unheard, tired of not being understood, and tired of catering to his ego every time his emotions went crazy (which was more often than not). I was completely frustrated, and I felt like I had put up with it for too long. I'd made up my mind in the beginning of the relationship that I wouldn't turn into a nag, but in our last two or three months together, I found myself becoming one because being nice hadn't worked for two years.

Because I was the sole breadwinner and tired of feeling alone in my efforts, I kicked him out. At that point, it made more sense for me to lead a calmer life without him because I would still be pulling the exact same amount of weight, just without all the emotional drama and frustration. Had he chosen to take the issues and apply a problem-solving attitude to them instead of an emotional one, that frustration could have been avoided or worked through.

So why was I so frustrated in the first place? A lack of balance. When I talk about balance, the concept is actually two-fold. On the one hand, you have balance as far as contributing to the relationship, the household, and the family dynamic, whether that be financially or in other ways. Back in the days of the nuclear family, the husband worked while the wife stayed home, took care of the family, cleaned the house, and cooked dinner. This was successful because each partner's role was very clear. Their tasks were outlined in a clear way and each person's responsibilities were understood by both parties.

These days, those roles have been thrown into complete chaos, between women being more ambitious in the work force and some men having no idea how to mow a lawn or work on a car; nothing is the way it once was. Whether this is a good thing or a bad thing is a matter of opinion; however, the lack of identifying responsibilities for each person in a relationship is harmful to the relationship as a whole. People are confused! They don't know what their responsibilities are anymore because they're taught they can do whatever they want to do with their lives.

This is why it's important to evaluate each person's responsibilities and contributions to the relationship and the household. I've created a short series of questions you can ask yourself as well as your partner in order to determine each person's roles and responsibilities for a balanced relationship and home life. Please write your answers on a separate sheet of paper; it might help sort some things out.

1. What do you expect from your partner?

2. What does your partner expect from you?

3. What do each of you feel comfortable doing around the house, in the yard, on the car, etc.?

4. Do you or your partner have a specific perception of what responsibilities a person of a certain gender *should* have?

5. If so, what are they and how do you work around it?

6. Do both of your ideas of what the other should contribute match up, or are they opposing ideas?

7. If they're opposing, how will you reach an agreement or compromise so that responsibilities are still being met?

8. If one of you is working and the other isn't, does that mean everything around the house falls on the person who isn't working? Why or why not?

9. Does the other person agree with this assessment? Why or why not?

10. Each of you get a piece of paper and write down what you feel your responsibilities are, what your partner's responsibilities are, and why this makes sense to you. Once you finish, exchange papers and go over what's agreeable and what isn't, then work on coming to an agreement on the things that cause conflict.

11. Once you come to an agreement, write it down as a responsibility list. Post this list of responsibilities on your fridge, a cabinet, or anywhere else that's easily accessible and easy to see.

Doing these exercises and writing a list of responsibilities will help keep arguments to a minimum and remind each of you what you need to do to keep the relationship (and the household) strong and happy. There's nothing more irritating than feeling like you have to do it all, especially with kids around as additional mess-makers. Add a pet or two in there and it really gets crazy!

So what's the other type of balance I'm talking about? This balance has more to do with time than with chores, but it is also extremely important. Though these things vary from one person to the next, it gets easier to learn what your partner needs when you can actually sit down and quantify the categories of balance.

Just as everyone has different love styles, everyone has different levels of need in each of the following categories to feel balanced.

There are four areas that need to be balanced out, and the amount of time and attention each area receives is different depending on each person. These were briefly covered in the second pillar, but I'd like to go into a bit more detail here.

Couple Time

This is the first category. Every couple needs to spend quality time together in order to remain close and become closer. The closer you become, the more likely you are to grow together and communicate well. Operative word: quality. It doesn't matter if you spend five hours or five days together nonstop – if there's no quality time, then you've really only spent five minutes.

Whatever your hobbies and interests may be, put in a little effort to do something you both enjoy for your couple time. This could be as simple as watching a movie or cooking together. Sometimes, it helps to do something your partner loves even if you don't necessarily enjoy it; they can do the same for you the next time you spend time together.

The main idea behind quality time is to feel connected to your partner. It doesn't have to be difficult or complicated. Back rubs, foot massages, snuggling while reading together or watching a movie, cooking together, playing a video game together… the options are endless and just depend on what you enjoy doing. If you enjoy having a conversation, then do that! Ultimately, it doesn't matter what you're doing, as long as you feel connected and are spending time together. That feeling of connectedness can happen through conversation or touch, bonding through doing an activity you both enjoy, or trying something new together that neither of you have tried but both want to.

Keep in mind that, no matter what you're doing, you can choose to have fun… or not. By listening to music while I clean, I am choosing to have fun with things I really don't enjoy a whole lot. Granted I do enjoy the end product after I clean, but the process itself? It's disgusting and sweaty and tedious, and I know I will never be done even when I finish the task at hand… because in a few days, it will start again. BUT! Listening to music makes it enjoyable and if I sing or dance while doing any of it, that suddenly makes it a million times easier.

Point? You choose whether you have fun or not.

So if your partner decides to take you out and do something "cheap" or "ordinary" or "mediocre," are you going to grumble and pout the whole time or appreciate the gesture for what it is… your partner reaching out? Talk – laugh – joke – enjoy yourself! Learn to take pleasure in the little things: good food, conversation, drinks, your partner's eyes and the way they look at you, their smile, their enthusiasm, the laughter you share even if the jokes are stupid, guessing people's jobs by the way they look, matching cars to couples… the possibilities are endless if you choose to see them that way.

Choose to have fun with your partner, even if date night isn't your idea of perfect every time.

Family Time

Whether you have kids or not, holidays are especially important to most families (I know they are to mine) and family time is essential! You may not have always gotten along with your parents, but you know that they brought you into this world, they raised you, they provided for you – and, most importantly, they want what's best for you. Doesn't this give them some clout? While some people get along well with their families, others don't – all understandable as we live in a world full of very different people. However, the family as a whole deserves respect. Part of that respect is spending time with them, whether you don't enjoy it or whether you do. I happen to be lucky enough that I do, and the holidays are fantastic at our house!

If you have kids, family time goes way beyond just the holidays. Family time goes into the daily routine. Kids don't care how you spend time with them – if you're broke, watch a movie on Netflix and eat popcorn in the living room (that's a big deal here because no kids are allowed to eat outside of the kitchen usually). Go to the park. Draw together, read a book together, play with clay together, play soccer in the back yard or at the park, ride bikes, you name it. There are a million options to spend time with the kids even if you're broke. If you're short on time, I can't help you out a whole lot; but if you're broke, just do something that's free. Lay on the deck and watch the clouds or do a journal day.

If you're have some money, more options open up. Go to the fair, the zoo, the kids' museum, a movie in the theater, the barber shop to have your hair cut together, go rent a boat and take it out on the lake, whatever you can think of. Go to a concert aimed at kids (or kids and adults alike). Go to a show of some kind. Go walk around the mall and browse the stores, maybe even have some food in the food court or play in the arcade. Go to the shooting range if that's what you're into! Go hunting or fishing.

> "I think togetherness is a very important ingredient to family life." –Barbara Bush

No matter what you decide to do with the family, being together helps. It helps the family be happy as a whole – even if your time spent together is simply eating dinner at the table for family dinner and then watching something on the TV together. The point is to nurture the family unit – you are a team, a unit, and are together for life. Why treat it like it's anything less than important?

Friend Time

Most people have friends… and even if they don't have "friends" plural, they have at least a friend other than their significant other.

Every guy needs a guy's night. Every girl needs a girl's night. I would say at a minimum once every two months, but that's me, and I'm a homebody. For most people, it's probably a minimum of every month or every two weeks. Whatever the case may be, everyone needs time with their friends! And unfortunately, a lot of people aren't the same around just their friends versus their significant other and their friends. This isn't true for everyone – but it can be expected, depending on the person's personality. But who cares? If they aren't cheating or doing something to hurt you in some way (if you trust them you'll know whether this is true or not), then what's the harm?

People going out: stay in contact via text. It's easy and not disruptive to a good time, but lets your partner know that you care, are thinking of them, and aren't doing anything they should be suspicious of. If they call, answer. If you miss the call, call them back when you see the missed call. It isn't rocket science… it's respect.

Now, sometimes people get jealous or upset even if you do things like this to show them that respect. That's their problem. If your significant other is freaking out because you aren't home yet, some conversations need to be had about this balance and your need for some kind of social life, even if that social life is rare.

If the socialization takes priority over the relationship or the respect thereof, however, then the problem might just be yours. Addiction to going out? I've been there. The lights, the people, the dancing, the drinks, the possibilities… it's intoxicating. On top of most likely being intoxicated. That is a direct breach of the balance, though. When is family time (including everyone)? When is couple time? If the other aspects of the balance aren't being met, you've got some serious issues that need to be addressed.

Alone Time

I absolutely adore my alone time, and at one point in my life, I had to fight tooth and nail to go spend two hours at the local coffee shop every two weeks or so and write in my journal by myself. That's probably a big part of the reason I value my alone time so much: I used to have to fight for it because of my then-partner's insecurity, overly jealous attitude, and controlling behavior.

Now, my alone time consists of reading, journaling, or watching something that the kids can't necessarily watch with me. I no longer feel the need to "escape" from my own home and actually prefer staying home to relax, especially since there are ample opportunities to spend time with the kids or just sit and write for a while. If I do journaling, my kids often join me. They like to write and draw in their journals, too, but we're all off in our own worlds, making this a perfect two-for-one activity: family time and alone time for all involved, all rolled into one activity.

"You cannot be lonely if you like the person you're alone with."
–Wayne Dyer

Even if you aren't a loner or don't need a whole lot of time to yourself, it's still important to maintain your own identity while in a relationship, which is the true purpose of alone time. Maybe you have a hobby that your partner has no interest in doing but you absolutely love. Now would be the time. Or maybe you just want a little privacy. I know that once kids are in the picture, privacy becomes harder and harder to come by, so if you want to just be alone and do something for yourself, that could also be considered alone time.

Maintaining your individuality is the point here. I can tell you from personal experience that losing yourself in order to please your partner is severely damaging in the long run. I remember a time after leaving an abusive relationship when I felt like I was a gray blob: no personality, no inspiration, because all I had thought about for several years was, "What will keep my partner from getting angry with me?" By the time I left that relationship, I had to do some serious soul searching and find who I was all over again.

To recap, the four categories of time balance are couple time, family time, friend time, and alone time. Ladies, don't fear guys' night out! Gentlemen, don't fear girls' night out! If you've done your due diligence for the relationship and have a healthy one, staying in touch throughout the night via text or calls is enough.

Don't fall into the trap of feeling like you need to be attached at the hip. If you or your partner need some time to yourselves or a night out, mention it. It's good to break the daily routine every once in a while.

Lastly, there's one more aspect of balance that should be covered.

The Balance of Extremes

Sometimes people fall into a vice they can't get out of or that damages them as well as the people around them. These can fall into several categories, but let's say in general they're addictions.

> "If one oversteps the bounds of moderation, the greatest pleasures cease to please." –Epictetus

An addiction can take almost any form. We've all heard of people who are workaholics, alcoholics, shopaholics, sexaholics, and so on. These behaviors are easy to fall into and difficult to climb out of, so be careful!

Not only are they addictions, but these behaviors tend to be extreme. They can also be damaging in some cases, although in other cases they aren't *quite* extreme enough to be a problem... yet.

What I want to focus on here is that, instead of having one extreme or the other, a happy medium should be found. For example, if your partner has an issue with overspending, maybe it's time to agree on an allowance of sorts. You definitely wouldn't give them access to your checking account – if they already have access, it's time to take it away, especially if they aren't earning their own money or they're putting your entire family in debt.

This is a problem that needs to be addressed. You don't want to say, "You can't spend any money at all," but you do want to limit the amount they're able to spend so that it doesn't get out of hand. Another option is to have them take a financial planning or budgeting course, which I'm sure is available online for a reasonable fee.

Any extreme behavior will eventually cause problems, so bringing it up to your partner (or them bringing it up to you) in a solution-oriented and positive way is the best way to deal with it. But again, if someone brings up an issue they're having, the response should be solution-oriented, not denial or lashing out.

When each person in a couple decides to work with their partner in constructive ways, it can work wonders for the relationship as well as the individuals involved. Helping each other to be better people is part of the dynamic that creates happy, healthy relationships. Give it a try with your partner – you deserve it!

The Tenth Pillar: Be Grateful

"Gratitude is not only the greatest of virtues, but the parent of all the others." –Marcus Tullius Cicero

This is probably the most important chapter of the book, which is why I saved it for last. I cannot tell you how important it is to say thank you and feel gratitude or appreciation for things others do. The importance is beyond words. What I *can* tell you is that being appreciative inspires more giving; being grateful inspires more gratitude. This in turn makes everyone feel happier and more appreciated. A simple thank you when someone does something for you or your family can work wonders.

If you do something for someone, do you expect something in return?

If your answer is yes, you're in the wrong state of mind.

The first time I learned this lesson – and it was fairly difficult because I felt very betrayed – was when I left a friend's house after staying with her and her parents one summer. She constantly complained about her life, so I suggested we do something about it. We "ran away;" we wandered around the neighborhood for a few hours and wound up going back (which I'd already figured would happen). I lost some of my most expensive, prized clothing for the experience, along with being punished through sleep deprivation and threatened with a knife by her mother. Overkill much?

When my mother came to pick me up the next day, we got about two blocks away before I burst into tears. I hadn't slept, I was hungry, I was threatened with a knife, and someone who I thought was my friend had completely betrayed me... not to mention all of the clothing I had bought with money I saved was suddenly gone. It felt like I'd worked to earn that money for nothing, and through no fault of my own (although I never "ran away" again in my life!).

Once I told my mom what happened, she was pretty peeved about it. Sleep deprivation is a form of torture, and her little girl had just been subjected to a knife-wielding psycho. She called her and chewed her out over the phone, threatening to call the police. I'm not sure what else the conversation entailed, but I was extremely grateful that my mom stood up for me and I really appreciated the gesture.

Anyway, the point is that my friend – the one who was complaining all the time – should have been grateful for the life she had. She had a roof over her head, food to eat, a family who loved her (even if they were dysfunctional), and overall, a good life. Before that last night, we had a lot of fun together. Playing cards, barbecuing, hanging out with friends… it was a good time, and I knew her life wasn't as bad as she complained that it was.

Gratitude is a powerful thing. It can shift your perspective in many cases, and lift your mood to a point where you don't overreact (as people often do) and maybe even find the good in a situation that initially makes you angry or hurts your feelings. For example, I should be grateful that my kids are so intelligent that they will call me out when I'm wrong, even though it makes me a bit angry when they do it. But really – they're kids and I'm wrong. How can I blame them for correcting me because I feel embarrassed when they do? That's a perfect time to reframe and allow myself to see their brilliance in the situation.

"Gratitude unlocks the fullness of life. It turns what we have into enough, and more. It turns denial into acceptance, chaos to order, confusion to clarity. It can turn a meal into a feast, a house into a home, a stranger into a friend."
–Melody Beattie

I've tried to help many people in my life. I have a soft spot for friends and will likely always try to help when I can. I feel bad when I don't. This has faded over the years from being a doormat to being more selective with whom I help, but it still doesn't change the fact that I feel bad when I can't help someone.

Now, here's the kicker:

Most of the time if I expect someone to pay me back (because they say they will) or give me some benefit in return (monetary or otherwise – babysitting, cleaning, whatever), I am disappointed severely. Why is that? Because I expect something. I expect something for what I gave out of supposed charity. That makes it NOT charity. That makes me the loaner and them the borrower. Now, I don't have the resources to make people go hunt these guys down and break their legs if they can't pay me back for a grand or three. Even if I did, that's just way too much! I'm not Al Capone.

That still doesn't make the entire situation okay.

Follow me here… I expected something in return, which meant I wasn't giving from my heart. That means it wasn't pure; I had made up my mind that, no matter what, I would hold this against that person for what they owed or some labor of the equivalent, forever – before I even "gave" them anything. And yes, I would settle for labor… do you know how hard it is trying to keep a clean house with three little kids and five cats trashing it all the time? OMG.

But, I digress.

The point is, this feeling of being owed, this feeling of entitlement, made me very bitter. It made me so bitter on several occasions, in fact, that I never spoke to those people again, and other times I didn't speak to them for years.

The words my mother said are priceless:

"Never lend anyone anything if you expect to get it back."

Had I listened to that from the start, I would still have all the books I treasured, movies and home videos, clothes, and money… but eventually, after seeing the pattern of people not repaying me, I realized that I could never loan anything to anyone if I needed it or expected it back.

That was how I learned to say no.

Just because you love someone doesn't mean they have to get their way all the time, nor does it mean you have to give in or bow to their wishes all the time. There is a time for the word no, believe me! Don't be a doormat.

Now, if someone does return a favor or do something nice, I don't expect it – and that means I'm pleasantly surprised and even more grateful than I would be if I had been expecting something. How cool is that? This feeling of gratitude, then, attracts more happy and good things to be grateful for. And usually those things are unexpected, because if you're unexpectedly grateful, you attract more of that to your life.

In a relationship, it's all about showing gratitude either in words or by doing something you know your partner will feel appreciative for.

Assuming both partners are somewhat emotionally healthy, the key to staying that way and nurturing the relationship fully is to encourage and nurture feelings of gratitude. Depending on what each of you enjoys, this can be kept very simple.

Let's say there's a chore chart and trade-offs are made daily so one person isn't constantly responsible for the same chores. That keeps it less mundane and repetitive. Even though the tasks have to be done and are expected, it doesn't hurt to make an exchange of something else in the evening, like a foot massage or cooking a meal.

It's impossible to keep things perfectly balanced all the time, but a simple, "thank you," works wonders, as long as you say it in a tone of voice that communicates sincere gratitude. A sarcastic, "thank you," will obviously inspire resentment and anger. Because we are constantly communicating on many levels (words are just the surface; there's also body language, tone of voice, inflection, mood emitted, and so on), remembering to be grateful allows us to communicate in a more positive way on all of those levels because we aren't secretly hiding a mountain of garbage under the proverbial rug and trying to fake our gratitude.

Fake gratitude doesn't work! There's this nifty little thing called instinct that humans have, and you'd be amazed how insightful our instincts can be if we trust them.

The beautiful thing about gratitude and a feeling of gratitude is that, even if you're miserable right now, you can begin to feel grateful for things in your life and about your partner *right now*. You can nurture this feeling and make it grow over time by meditating or simply doing a run-down of three to five things you're grateful for once every day. Or you can do what many have suggested and keep a gratitude journal. Whatever you choose to do, it will begin to shift your state of mind and allow you to be more of the best of who you truly are.

"As we express our gratitude, we must never forget that the highest appreciation is not to utter words, but to live by them."
–John F. Kennedy

Having said that, imagine a relationship with the person you love where you sit down together for five to ten minutes a day and talk only about things you are grateful for in the other person. Traits you love about your partner, things they did for you that day, maybe a memory you both have together that brings you joy – just doing that little exercise with sincerity can work wonders for your relationship. This is not to say that the relationship will be perfect or won't have problems – it would be naïve to think that – but it will definitely become a happier relationship.

Final Thoughts

There are many books you can buy that go into much more detail about all of these aspects of relationships. However, this is a good starting point for those of us who have had issues with building lasting relationships and have maybe had to learn the hard way at times.

My background as far as relationships go is multifaceted; I grew up moving from one place to the next, so ending friendships and relationships became easier for me than most, while sticking to it and committing became more difficult. I was always searching for perfection, and in my early years, when that perfection proved to be nonexistent in a partner, I ended the relationship altogether.

Unfortunately, that meant starting all over again.

There are so many things to consider when being with someone that it can be overwhelming, especially if you're like me and feel happy being single. I've had relationships so horrible that I would rather stay alone for the rest of my life than with that person, hands down. However, I've also had happy relationships that wound up ending because of a mistake or something as simple as a lie or a psychological disorder that was beyond my help.

I hope to reach others who have had issues with the relationship basics that are necessary to have a happy relationship, as well as those who have maybe been in relationships for all the wrong reasons. The ideas and life lessons in this book are meant to give a solid foundation to those who have struggled with finding happiness and stability with a partner.

Having said that, I hope you enjoyed the book and that you pass it on to those who may need it!

Recommended Resources

Unlimited Power by Anthony Robbins

The Secret by Rhonda Byrne

Sacred Selfishness by Bud Harris

Your Elephant's Under Threat by John Mulry

Do You Want to Drive or Do You Want to Bitch? by Sheldon Wayne Moss

110 Ways to Boost Your Self-Esteem by Henriette Eiby Christensen

110 Ways to Change Your Mind by Henriette Eiby Christensen

The Ten Pillars of a Happy Relationship
Jennifer-Crystal Johnson

About the Author

Jennifer-Crystal Johnson is a single mother of three children and the owner/operator of Broken Publications, an independent book publishing company (brokenpublications.com). Her fiction and non-fiction work has appeared in magazines and on websites for several years. To help support her family and her business, she does freelance writing and editing work, along with consulting and eBook formatting. She is currently the editor in chief of Plaid for Women Publishing, and Managing Editor at *phati'tude* Literary Magazine.

Apart from her writing and editing endeavors, Jen is a domestic violence advocate. She publishes an anthology about domestic violence called Soul Vomit as well as creating personal development courses to help victims and survivors to overcome the emotional aftermath of living through domestic abuse. When finalized, those courses can be found at www.SoulVomit.com.

For more on Jen, her business, or to read her blog, please visit www.JenniferCrystalJohnson.com.

Relevant Websites:

www.JenniferCrystalJohnson.com
www.BrokenPublications.com
www.SoulVomit.com

To Befriend or Follow Me on Facebook:

www.Facebook.com/BrokenPoetJen
www.Facebook.com/JenniferCrystalJohnson
www.Facebook.com/BrokenPublications
www.Facebook.com/SoulVomitAnthology

www.ingramcontent.com/pod-product-compliance
Lightning Source LLC
Chambersburg PA
CBHW071600040426
42452CB00008B/1240